Advanced Guide To

Python
Syntax

Global Institute of Science & Technology

"Building Blocks" is an educational series that is guided by the practice of Dr. Lael A. Alexander in order to encourage elemental literacy in American Students.

Global Institute of Science and Technology
Tulsa, Oklahoma Published by Penguin & Rook LLC

Advanced Guide To

Python

Syntax

Global Institute of Science & Technology

Book Title: Building Blocks
Subtitle (optional): Advance Guide to *Python Syntax*
Author: Dr. Lael A. Alexander
Publisher Information: Penguin & Rook LLC
Edition: First Edition
Date of Publication: March 17, 2024

Copyright Page

- **ISBN:** TBD
- **Publisher Information:** Penguin & Rook LLC

Dedication

For those who dream of a decentralized future where technology empowers everyone equally.

Table of Contents

Preface for Python Syntax

For decades, Python has been at the forefront of software development, powering everything from web applications to artificial intelligence, data science, and automation. Its simplicity, versatility, and strong community support have made it one of the most popular programming languages in the world.

This book takes you on a journey through Python's evolution, from a general-purpose scripting language to a dominant force in machine learning, web development, and scalable enterprise solutions. Whether you're looking to build RESTful APIs, integrate Python with modern front-end frameworks, or leverage its power in blockchain, AI, and automation, this book will provide you with the knowledge and confidence to do so.

Introduction to Python Syntax

Python is a high-level, server-side programming language designed for efficiency, readability, and versatility. In this book, you'll learn how to harness Python's capabilities to interact with databases, create secure APIs, and build scalable applications that can power modern web, AI, and automation systems. Starting with the fundamentals, this book gradually introduces advanced topics, including Python frameworks like Django and Flask, data processing with Pandas, and integrating Python with cloud services and AI models.

The practical examples in this book are tailored toward real-world applications, helping you not only learn the syntax and tools but also understand how to apply them effectively in various domains.

Notes from the Author on Python

Some may see Python as just another scripting language, but its adaptability has made it an essential tool in data science, web development, AI, and automation. I have used Python to bridge traditional web systems with AI models, blockchain, and cloud-based architectures. My goal with this book is to showcase how Python remains one of the most powerful and relevant programming languages for modern development, particularly for scalable applications, backend logic, and data-driven systems.

Chapter 1: Introduction to Python

What is Python?

Python is a high-level, interpreted programming language that has gained immense popularity since its inception in the late 1980s. Created by Guido van Rossum and first released in 1991, Python was designed with an emphasis on code readability and simplicity, making it an ideal choice for both beginners and experienced programmers. Its syntax is clear and intuitive, allowing developers to express concepts in fewer lines of code compared to languages like C++ or Java. This accessibility has contributed significantly to Python's widespread adoption across various domains, from web development to data analysis.

One of the standout features of Python is its versatility. It supports multiple programming paradigms, including procedural, object-oriented, and functional programming. This flexibility allows coders to select the best approach for their projects, whether they are developing sophisticated web applications, automating tedious tasks, or designing complex machine learning algorithms. Python’s extensive standard library and a vast ecosystem of third-party packages further enhance its capabilities, enabling developers to tackle a wide array of challenges with ease.

In the realm of data analysis, Python has established itself as a powerhouse. Libraries such as Pandas, NumPy, and Matplotlib empower data scientists and analysts to manipulate, process, and visualize data efficiently. This functionality is invaluable for making data-driven decisions in various industries, from finance to healthcare. Additionally, Python's integration with tools like Jupyter Notebooks allows for interactive data exploration, making it a favorite among academics and researchers who require a seamless workflow for their experiments.

For web development, Python offers robust frameworks such as Django and Flask, which simplify the process of building dynamic websites and web applications. These frameworks provide essential tools for developers, such as routing, templating, and database integration, enabling them to focus on creating rich user experiences. The growing demand for web applications has made Python a go-to choice for startups and established companies alike, as it allows for rapid development and deployment.

Beyond web development and data analysis, Python is also making significant strides in areas like machine learning, artificial intelligence, and automation. Libraries such as TensorFlow and scikit-learn provide powerful tools for building predictive models and deploying neural networks. Meanwhile, its capabilities in automation and scripting make it a favorite among system administrators and DevOps professionals. With the rise of the Internet of Things (IoT) and the increasing need for cybersecurity solutions, Python's versatility ensures that it remains at the forefront of technological innovation, proving itself to be an essential language for coders, computer science students, and tech enthusiasts alike.

History and Evolution of Python

Python's history began in the late 1980s when Guido van Rossum, a Dutch programmer, started working on a new scripting language as a successor to the ABC language. The primary goal was to create a language that would be easy to read and write, while also being powerful enough to handle complex programming tasks. Van Rossum aimed to incorporate features from other programming languages, such as C and Modula-3, to enhance the functionality and usability of Python. The first official version, Python 0.9.0, was released in February 1991, introducing core features such as functions, exception handling, and the core data types of list and dictionary.

Over the years, Python evolved significantly, with the release of version 1.0 in January 1994 marking a notable milestone. This version included new features such as tools for module creation and the introduction of new data types. The growth of the internet during the mid-1990s played a critical role in Python's adoption, as developers began using it for web development, leveraging frameworks like Zope for building dynamic web applications. This era marked the beginning of Python's journey into various domains, demonstrating its versatility and capability to handle a wide range of programming tasks.

The introduction of Python 2.0 in October 2000 brought an array of new features, including list comprehensions and a garbage collection system, which improved memory management. This version solidified Python's reputation as a reliable language for both beginners and experienced programmers. Python 2.x gained widespread use in academia and industry, especially in fields such as data analysis and scientific computing. However, as technology advanced and the programming landscape evolved, the need for a more robust and efficient version became apparent.

Python 3.0 was released in December 2008, introducing significant changes that emphasized a cleaner and more consistent language design. While Python 3 was not backward compatible with Python 2, it incorporated various enhancements aimed at improving performance and usability. Features such as print function syntax, improved Unicode support, and better handling of integers and strings made Python 3 more appealing for modern applications. This transition marked a pivotal moment in Python's evolution, as it shifted the focus toward more complex domains like machine learning, artificial intelligence, and automation.

Today, Python stands as one of the most popular programming languages globally, embraced by coders, computer science students, and technology enthusiasts alike. Its extensive libraries and frameworks, such as

Pandas for data analysis, Flask for web development, and TensorFlow for machine learning, have positioned Python as a leading choice across various niches. The ongoing development and community support ensure that Python continues to adapt and thrive in the ever-changing landscape of technology, making it an essential tool for anyone interested in coding or exploring advanced applications like IoT and cybersecurity.

Setting Up Your Python Environment

Setting up your Python environment is a crucial step for any coder, computer science student, or technology enthusiast eager to dive into the world of Python programming. The first decision you'll need to make is which version of Python to install. As of October 2023, Python 3.x is the recommended version, as it includes a wealth of features and improvements over its predecessor, Python 2.x. Downloading the latest stable release from the official Python website ensures that you are equipped with the most up-to-date tools and libraries. It is also essential to verify that your operating system is compatible with the chosen version, whether you are using Windows, macOS, or a Linux distribution.

After installing Python, the next step is to configure your development environment. Integrated Development Environments (IDEs) such as PyCharm, Visual Studio Code, and Jupyter Notebook are popular choices among Python developers. Each IDE offers unique features tailored to different programming needs, from web development to data analysis. For instance, Jupyter

Notebook is particularly favored in data science and machine learning due to its interactive coding capabilities, while PyCharm excels in supporting web development and software engineering with its robust debugging tools. Selecting the right IDE will significantly enhance your coding experience and productivity.

Package management is another key aspect of setting up your Python environment. Python's package manager, pip, allows you to install and manage third-party libraries that can extend the functionality of your projects. Popular libraries for specific niches include NumPy and pandas for data analysis, Flask and Django for web development, and TensorFlow and scikit-learn for machine learning. To ensure that your projects remain organized and dependencies are managed effectively, consider using virtual environments with tools like venv or conda. This practice isolates project environments, preventing conflicts between different package versions and dependencies.

Configuring your environment variables is also important for optimal performance. Setting the PATH variable allows your operating system to locate Python and its associated tools without necessitating full directory paths. This step simplifies the process of running scripts and accessing installed packages via the command line. Additionally, taking the time to customize your terminal or command prompt settings can improve your workflow. Whether you prefer using PowerShell, Command Prompt, or a Unix shell, ensuring that your environment is tailored to your preferences will make your coding sessions more efficient.

Finally, it's advisable to familiarize yourself with version control systems like Git. Integrating Git into your Python projects enhances collaboration and enables you to track changes effectively. Platforms like GitHub or GitLab not only provide repositories for your code but also facilitate project management and team collaboration. By mastering these tools early on, you build a foundation that will serve you well as you explore various niches such as web development, machine learning, or automation. Setting up a robust Python environment is the first step toward unlocking your potential as a programmer and tackling diverse challenges across multiple domains.

Basic Syntax and Data Types

In Python, basic syntax serves as the foundation for writing and understanding code. Unlike many programming languages that require extensive boilerplate code, Python emphasizes readability and simplicity. This design philosophy enables beginners to grasp concepts quickly, allowing them to focus on problem-solving rather than getting bogged down by complex syntax rules. The use of indentation to define code blocks is a prime example of Python's unique syntax, which enhances code clarity and enforces a structured approach. Understanding this syntax is crucial for anyone looking to leverage Python in various domains, from web development to data analysis.

Data types in Python are fundamental components that allow programmers to store and manipulate data efficiently. The language supports several built-in data types, including integers, floats, strings, and booleans. Integers and floats are used for numerical calculations, while strings are employed for text manipulation. Booleans, representing True or False values, are essential for decision-making in programming. Each data type serves specific use cases, and knowing when to use each type is vital for effective coding. In addition to these basic types, Python also offers complex data structures like lists, tuples, sets, and dictionaries, which allow for more sophisticated data organization.

Lists are one of the most versatile data types in Python, enabling the storage of ordered collections of items. They can contain elements of different types and support various operations, such as adding, removing, and slicing elements. Tuples, on the other hand, are similar to lists but are immutable, meaning their contents cannot be changed after creation. This property makes tuples useful for fixed data collections. Sets provide a unique collection of unordered items, while dictionaries allow for key-value pair storage, facilitating efficient data retrieval. Understanding these data structures is essential for any aspiring coder, as they form the building blocks for more complex data manipulations and analyses.

Python also provides dynamic typing, which means that the data type of a variable is determined at runtime rather than in advance. This flexibility allows programmers to write more agile code, as they can easily change the type of a variable without declaring it explicitly. However, this feature also necessitates a strong understanding of the types being used to avoid runtime errors. It is beneficial for beginners to practice identifying and converting data types, particularly when engaging in activities such as data analysis or machine learning, where data types can significantly influence outcomes and model performance.

As beginners become comfortable with Python's syntax and data types, they will find themselves better equipped to tackle a variety of projects across different domains. Whether developing web applications, automating mundane tasks, or analyzing complex datasets, a solid grasp of these foundational concepts is crucial. Mastering basic syntax and data types not only enhances coding skills but also builds confidence in using Python for advanced applications in fields like artificial intelligence, cybersecurity, and the Internet of Things. As learners progress, they will discover that these concepts are not just theoretical; they are the keys to unlocking Python's vast potential in the technology landscape.

Writing Your First Python Program

Writing your first Python program is an exciting milestone in your coding journey. Python is renowned for its simplicity and readability, making it an ideal language for beginners. To get started, you'll need to install Python on your machine. The official Python website offers easy-to-follow instructions for downloading the latest version, which includes an integrated development environment (IDE) known as IDLE. This IDE allows you to write, debug, and execute your code efficiently. Once installed, you can launch IDLE and create a new file where you will write your first program.

The quintessential first program for many coders is the classic "Hello, World!" example. This simple program serves as a rite of passage, introducing you to the syntax of Python. In IDLE, you can write the code by typing `print("Hello, World!")`. This command instructs the interpreter to display the text in quotation marks on the screen. After writing the code, save the file with a `.py` extension, which denotes that it is a Python script. To run the program, you can either use the run command within IDLE or execute it from the terminal or command prompt by navigating to the file's directory and typing `python filename.py`.

As you gain confidence with basic commands, you can explore more complex concepts such as variables, data types, and control structures. Variables allow you to store information that can be manipulated later in your program. For example, you can create a variable called `greeting` and assign it the string "Hello, World!" by writing `greeting = "Hello, World!"`. You can then use `print(greeting)` to display it. Understanding data types—such as strings, integers, and lists—will enable you to handle different kinds of information effectively. Control structures like loops and conditional statements will further empower you to create dynamic and interactive programs.

Python's versatility makes it suitable for various applications, from data analysis to web development, machine learning, and beyond. As you write your first program, consider how you can apply Python to your specific interests. For instance, if you are drawn to data analysis, you might want to explore libraries like Pandas and NumPy after mastering the basics. If web development fascinates you, you can experiment with frameworks like Flask or Django. Understanding the foundational elements of Python will provide you with the tools necessary to delve into these specialized areas.

Finally, remember that writing code is an iterative process. You may encounter errors or bugs initially, which is a normal part of programming. Use these moments as learning opportunities to improve your debugging skills. The Python community is vast and supportive, with numerous resources available online, including forums, tutorials, and documentation. Engaging with this community can enhance your learning experience and provide valuable insights as you embark on your programming journey. With practice and persistence, writing your first Python program will be just the beginning of your exploration into the world of coding.

Chapter 2: Python for Data Analysis

Introduction to Data Analysis

Data analysis is an essential skill in today's technology-driven world, enabling individuals to extract meaningful insights from vast amounts of information. As coders and computer science students, understanding how to manipulate and analyze data using Python opens doors to various applications, ranging from web development to machine learning. The ability to translate raw data into actionable knowledge is invaluable, especially in fields like artificial intelligence, scientific computing, and cybersecurity, where data is the foundation of innovation and decision-making.

Python has emerged as a leading programming language for data analysis due to its simplicity and versatility. Its extensive libraries, such as Pandas, NumPy, and Matplotlib, provide powerful tools for data manipulation, statistical analysis, and visualization. These libraries help streamline the data analysis process, allowing users to focus on deriving insights rather than getting bogged down by complex coding. The ease of integrating Python with other technologies further enhances its applicability across various domains, making it a preferred choice for both beginners and experienced developers.

In the realm of data analysis, understanding different data types and structures is crucial. Data can be categorized into various formats, such as structured, unstructured, and semi-structured, each requiring specific handling techniques. Python offers a variety of data structures, including lists, dictionaries, and data frames, which are instrumental in organizing and processing data efficiently. By gaining proficiency in these structures, coders can develop robust data analysis workflows that can handle real-world data challenges effectively.

Visualization is another critical aspect of data analysis that cannot be overlooked. The ability to present data visually helps in identifying trends, patterns, and outliers, making complex information more digestible. Python's visualization libraries, such as Matplotlib and Seaborn, empower users to create a wide range of static and interactive plots. This capability not only aids in data interpretation but also enhances communication with stakeholders who may not be familiar with intricate data concepts.

Ultimately, mastering data analysis with Python equips coders and computer science students with a competitive edge in their respective fields. As companies increasingly rely on data-driven decision-making, the demand for professionals skilled in data analysis continues to rise. Whether you are interested in web development, machine learning, or scientific research, a solid foundation in data analysis will enhance your coding capabilities and open up numerous career opportunities in the ever-evolving tech landscape.

Libraries for Data Analysis: NumPy and Pandas

In the realm of data analysis, two libraries stand out as essential tools for Python programmers: NumPy and Pandas. NumPy, short for Numerical Python, is a powerful library that provides support for large, multi-dimensional arrays and matrices, along with a collection of mathematical functions to operate on these arrays. This library is particularly useful for numerical computations and serves as the foundation for many other scientific computing libraries in Python. By utilizing NumPy, coders can efficiently perform operations on large datasets, making it an indispensable resource for anyone working with data.

Pandas, on the other hand, is specifically designed for data manipulation and analysis. It introduces two primary data structures: Series and DataFrame. A Series is essentially a one-dimensional array that can hold various data types, while a DataFrame is a two-dimensional, tabular data structure, akin to a spreadsheet or SQL table. Pandas allows users to easily manipulate, filter, and analyze data, making it a go-to library for data wrangling tasks. Its intuitive syntax and powerful functions enable users to perform complex data transformations with minimal code, significantly enhancing productivity and efficiency in data analysis workflows.

The integration of NumPy and Pandas provides a robust framework for performing data analysis in Python. For instance, users can leverage NumPy's powerful array operations to perform numerical calculations on large datasets, and then seamlessly transition to Pandas for data manipulation and visualization. This synergy allows coders to handle everything from simple data tasks to sophisticated analyses without the need for multiple programming languages or tools. Furthermore, both libraries are designed to work efficiently with large datasets, making them suitable for applications in diverse fields such as finance, healthcare, and scientific research.

One of the standout features of Pandas is its ability to handle missing data. In real-world datasets, missing values are common, and Pandas provides a variety of methods for identifying and dealing with these gaps. Users can easily drop missing values, fill them with specific values or statistical measures, or interpolate them based on surrounding data. This functionality is crucial for maintaining the integrity of analyses and ensuring that results are reliable and accurate. By effectively managing missing data, coders can improve the quality of their analyses and derive more meaningful insights from their datasets.

In conclusion, mastering NumPy and Pandas is essential for anyone looking to delve into data analysis using Python. These libraries not only simplify the process of data manipulation but also enhance the overall analytical capabilities of Python. As the demand for data-driven decision-making continues to grow across various sectors, acquiring proficiency in NumPy and Pandas will empower coders, students, and technology enthusiasts to leverage the full potential of Python for data analysis, paving the way for innovative solutions in fields ranging from machine learning to scientific computing.

Data Manipulation and Cleaning

Data manipulation and cleaning are crucial steps in the data analysis process, especially when working with Python. For coders and computer science students, understanding how to effectively manage and transform data can significantly enhance the quality of insights derived from datasets. Raw data is often messy, containing inconsistencies, missing values, and irrelevant information. By using Python libraries such as Pandas and NumPy, users can streamline these processes, making it easier to prepare data for analysis or machine learning tasks.

One of the primary tasks in data cleaning involves identifying and handling missing data. Missing values can skew results and lead to inaccurate conclusions if not addressed properly. Python provides various techniques to handle missing data, including imputation, where missing values are replaced with statistical measures like mean or median, or removal, where rows or columns with missing data are deleted. Understanding these techniques enables coders to make informed decisions on how to treat incomplete datasets, ultimately improving the robustness of their analyses.

Data manipulation also involves transforming and reshaping datasets to fit specific analytical needs. This includes operations such as filtering, aggregating, and merging datasets. For instance, using Pandas, users can easily filter data based on certain criteria, aggregate data to summarize information, and merge multiple datasets to create a comprehensive view of the data landscape. These manipulation techniques are essential for preparing data in a format suitable for visualization or further statistical analysis, which is particularly valuable in fields like web development and machine learning.

Another important aspect of data cleaning is dealing with outliers and inconsistencies. Outliers can distort statistical analyses and lead to misleading interpretations. Python offers tools for identifying and managing outliers, such as the Z-score method or the IQR method, which can help coders decide whether to exclude these values or treat them differently. Additionally, standardizing formats—such as dates or categorical variables—ensures that data is uniformly structured, which simplifies further processing and enhances the accuracy of the results.

Finally, the practice of documenting the data cleaning process is essential for reproducibility and transparency. Coders should maintain clear records of the steps taken during data manipulation and cleaning, including any changes made to the original dataset. This practice not only helps in future projects but also aids collaboration with other team members who may need to understand the rationale behind certain decisions. By mastering data manipulation and cleaning techniques in Python, coders and computer science students can significantly elevate their data analysis skills, making them valuable contributors in various technological domains, from automation and scripting to artificial intelligence and IoT.

Data Visualization with Matplotlib and Seaborn

Data visualization is a crucial aspect of data analysis, providing a means to present complex data in a more understandable and visually appealing format. In the realm of Python programming, Matplotlib and Seaborn are two powerful libraries that facilitate this process. Matplotlib is the foundational library for creating static, animated, and interactive visualizations in Python. It offers a wide range of plotting functions and customization options, making it a go-to tool for many data analysts and scientists. Seaborn, built on top of Matplotlib, provides a high-level interface for drawing attractive statistical graphics. It simplifies the process of creating complex visualizations and improves the aesthetics of the plots.

When working with Matplotlib, users can create various types of plots, such as line plots, bar charts, histograms, and scatter plots, among others. The library's versatility allows users to customize nearly every aspect of a plot, including titles, labels, colors, and styles. For example, one can easily create a simple line plot to visualize data trends over time by using the `plot()` function. With just a few lines of code, coders can generate insightful visual representations that can enhance their data analysis and storytelling capabilities.

Seaborn enhances the experience of data visualization by providing a higher-level interface that abstracts some of the complexities found in Matplotlib. It is particularly well-suited for statistical data visualization, offering built-in themes and color palettes that can make plots more visually appealing and easier to interpret. For instance, Seaborn's `sns.scatterplot()` function allows users to create scatter plots with additional features like color coding and size adjustments based on data variables. This feature is incredibly useful for analyzing relationships between multiple variables in a dataset, making it a favorite among data analysts and scientists.

Both libraries can be used in tandem to create comprehensive and visually stunning visualizations. By leveraging the capabilities of Matplotlib and Seaborn, users can produce detailed reports and presentations that effectively communicate their findings. This combination is particularly valuable in fields such as machine learning and scientific computing, where the ability to visualize data patterns and model performance can significantly influence decision-making and strategy development. Moreover, the seamless integration of these libraries with other Python libraries like Pandas makes it easy to import, manipulate, and visualize data in a streamlined workflow.

As technology continues to evolve, the importance of data visualization will only increase. Mastering tools like Matplotlib and Seaborn will empower coders, computer science students, and technology enthusiasts to harness the full potential of their data. Whether it is for web development, automation, or even game development, the ability to create informative and aesthetically pleasing visual representations of data can enhance any project. By investing time in learning these visualization libraries, aspiring data scientists and programmers can significantly boost their skill set and improve the impact of their work.

Real-world Data Analysis Projects

Real-world data analysis projects serve as a practical application of the theoretical knowledge acquired in Python programming. These projects bridge the gap between classroom learning and hands-on experience, allowing coders and students to tackle genuine problems using data-driven methodologies. Engaging in such projects not only enhances coding skills but also fosters a deeper understanding of data manipulation, visualization, and interpretation, which are essential skills in today's technology-driven world.

One common type of data analysis project involves exploring public datasets available from various sources, such as government databases, academic institutions, or open-source repositories. For instance, a project might focus on analyzing COVID-19 data to identify trends in infection rates across different regions. By leveraging libraries like Pandas, Matplotlib, and Seaborn, coders can clean the dataset, perform exploratory data analysis, and create visualizations that effectively communicate their findings. This type of project exemplifies how Python can be used to derive insights from complex datasets, making it an invaluable skill for aspiring data analysts and scientists.

Another exciting avenue for real-world data analysis projects is social media data analysis. Coders can utilize APIs provided by platforms like Twitter or Instagram to gather data on user interactions, trends, and sentiments. This analysis can reveal valuable insights into public opinion or consumer behavior, which businesses and organizations can leverage for strategic decision-making. Utilizing Python's libraries such as Tweepy for accessing Twitter data or TextBlob for sentiment analysis, students can conduct comprehensive analyses that reflect real-world applicability and relevance.

In the realm of business intelligence, analyzing sales data can provide significant insights into customer preferences and market trends. A project could involve examining historical sales data to predict future sales using machine learning algorithms. By employing libraries such as Scikit-learn, individuals can build predictive models that help businesses optimize inventory management and marketing strategies. This type of project not only demonstrates the power of Python in data analysis but also showcases the importance of data in driving business success.

Finally, data analysis projects can also be geared towards environmental studies, such as analyzing climate change data. Coders can work with datasets that track temperature changes, carbon emissions, or deforestation rates. By visualizing these trends and correlating them with human activities, students can provide critical insights into the challenges posed by climate change. Utilizing Python's capabilities for data analysis enables students to contribute meaningfully to discussions about sustainability and environmental responsibility, reinforcing the notion that coding can be a powerful tool for societal impact.

Chapter 3: Python for Web Development

Overview of Web Development

Web development is a multifaceted domain that encompasses the creation and maintenance of websites and web applications. It involves a combination of programming, design, and user experience considerations to build platforms that are both functional and visually appealing. At its core, web development can be divided into two primary areas: front-end development, which focuses on what users interact with directly, and back-end development, which deals with the server-side logic and database interactions. Understanding these areas is crucial for anyone looking to dive into web development, especially for those interested in utilizing Python as a primary language.

Front-end development primarily involves the use of languages such as HTML, CSS, and JavaScript. HTML (Hypertext Markup Language) structures the content on the web, CSS (Cascading Style Sheets) styles that content, and JavaScript adds interactivity to web pages. Together, these technologies create the user interface that visitors interact with when they navigate a website. While Python is not traditionally used for front-end development, frameworks like Django and Flask can facilitate the integration of back-end functionality into front-end applications, allowing for a more seamless experience.

On the back end, web development relies on server-side programming languages, database management, and application logic. Python has emerged as a powerful tool for back-end development, thanks to its simplicity and versatility. Frameworks like Django and Flask allow developers to build robust applications rapidly and efficiently. These frameworks support the Model-View-Template (MVT) architecture, which helps in organizing code and separating concerns, making it easier to manage complex applications. Additionally, Python's extensive libraries and tools enhance its capability to handle tasks such as user authentication, data storage, and API integration.

Another significant aspect of web development is the importance of responsive design, which ensures that websites function well across various devices and screen sizes. With the rise of mobile browsing, creating a responsive website has become a necessity. This requires a deep understanding of how to use CSS frameworks like Bootstrap or utilities like media queries to adapt the layout and design dynamically. For Python developers, this means not only mastering back-end skills but also collaborating with front-end developers to create cohesive and user-friendly experiences.

In conclusion, web development is a crucial skill set for anyone interested in technology and programming. For Python enthusiasts, the combination of front-end and back-end development offers a wide range of possibilities, from creating simple web pages to building complex web applications. As the digital landscape continues to evolve, understanding the principles of web development and how to leverage Python will empower coders and computer science students to contribute to innovative projects and solutions in the tech industry.

Frameworks: Flask vs Django

Flask and Django are two of the most popular web frameworks in the Python ecosystem, each offering unique features that cater to different development needs. Flask is a micro-framework that provides the essentials for web development, allowing developers the flexibility to choose their tools and libraries. It is lightweight and modular, making it an excellent choice for small to medium-sized applications or for developers who prefer a more hands-on approach. This minimalistic design encourages experimentation and customization, which can be particularly appealing for those who are just starting with web development and want to understand the underlying mechanics.

On the other hand, Django is a high-level framework that promotes rapid development and clean, pragmatic design. It comes with numerous built-in features, such as an ORM, authentication system, and an admin panel, which can significantly speed up the development process. This framework follows the "batteries-included" philosophy, meaning it provides a wide range of tools out of the box. For coders who are looking to build more complex applications quickly, such as content management systems or e-commerce sites, Django offers a robust solution that minimizes the need for additional integrations.

The choice between Flask and Django often comes down to project requirements and personal preferences. Flask's simplicity allows for quick prototyping, making it ideal for projects that require rapid iteration and testing. Developers can easily add or modify components without being constrained by a rigid structure. In contrast, Django's comprehensive feature set is beneficial for larger projects where speed and scalability are critical. Its built-in functionalities can save time and resources, allowing teams to focus on developing unique features rather than reinventing the wheel.

In terms of community and ecosystem, both frameworks are well-supported with extensive documentation and a wealth of third-party libraries. Flask's community tends to be more focused on microservices and lightweight applications, while Django's community often engages in discussions surrounding larger, full-featured applications. This difference influences the types of resources, tutorials, and plugins available, making it essential for developers to consider their specific needs when choosing between the two. Additionally, the choice of framework can influence the learning curve for beginners, as Django's comprehensive nature may require more upfront learning compared to Flask's straightforward approach.

Ultimately, the decision between Flask and Django should align with the goals of the project and the preferences of the developers involved. For those interested in exploring Python for web development, both frameworks provide valuable experiences that can enhance understanding and proficiency in coding. Whether one opts for the minimalist approach of Flask or the robust capabilities of Django, each framework offers a pathway to creating dynamic web applications, allowing developers to unlock the potential of Python in a practical and engaging way.

Building Your First Web Application

Building your first web application is an exciting milestone that can significantly enhance your programming skills and broaden your understanding of how the web functions. Python, with its simplicity and powerful libraries, is an excellent choice for web development. This subchapter will guide you through the essential steps to create your first web application using Python, focusing on the Flask framework, which is lightweight and beginner-friendly. By the end, you'll have a functional web application and a solid foundation to explore more complex projects.

To begin, you'll need to install Flask, which can be easily done using pip, Python's package installer. Open your terminal and run the command "pip install Flask." Once installed, create a new directory for your project and set up a simple file structure. Within this directory, create a new Python file, typically named app.py. This file will contain the main code of your web application. Understanding the basic structure of a Flask application is key; you'll import Flask, create an instance of the Flask class, and define routes that will correspond to different pages of your application.

Next, it's time to define your first route. In the app.py file, you can create a simple web page by defining a function that returns a string or HTML. Use the "@app.route('/') decorator to bind your function to the root URL. When you run your application by executing "python app.py" and navigate to http://127.0.0.1:5000/ in your web browser, you'll see the output of your function displayed as a web page. This initial step is crucial as it introduces you to how URL routing works in web applications.

As you develop your web application further, you can incorporate templates to render dynamic HTML content. Flask supports Jinja2 templating, allowing you to separate your Python logic from HTML. Create a "templates" folder in your project directory and add an HTML file, like index.html. Modify your route to render this HTML template using Flask's render_template function. This practice not only enhances your application's aesthetics but also makes it easier to manage larger projects as you separate concerns effectively.

Finally, consider adding interactivity to your web application by utilizing forms and handling user input. Flask simplifies this process with the request object, which allows you to access data submitted through forms. Create a simple form in your HTML template, and set up a route to handle the data when the form is submitted. This interaction illustrates the dynamic nature of web applications and solidifies your understanding of how front-end and back-end components work together. By completing these steps, you have not only built your first web application but also laid the groundwork for exploring more advanced topics in Python web development.

Working with APIs

Working with APIs is a crucial skill for anyone delving into the world of programming, especially for those involved in diverse fields such as web development, data analysis, and machine learning. An API, or Application Programming Interface, serves as a bridge between different software applications, allowing them to communicate and share data seamlessly. In the context of Python, APIs enable developers to leverage external functionalities, access data from various services, and enhance their applications without having to build everything from scratch. Understanding how to interact with APIs opens up a wealth of possibilities for enhancing projects across various domains, from automating tasks to integrating machine learning models.

To begin working with APIs in Python, it is essential to familiarize yourself with HTTP requests, as most APIs operate over this protocol. Python's `requests` library simplifies the process of making these requests, enabling users to retrieve or send data to external services easily. When interacting with an API, you typically perform operations such as GET to retrieve data, POST to send data, PUT to update existing data, and DELETE to remove data. By mastering these methods, you can effectively communicate with a wide range of APIs, whether they are public services like weather data or private APIs for proprietary systems.

Authentication is another key aspect of working with APIs. Many services require users to authenticate themselves to ensure that only authorized applications can access their data. This can involve using API keys, OAuth tokens, or other methods of identification. Understanding the authentication process is vital for any developer looking to utilize APIs securely and effectively. In Python, libraries such as `requests-oauthlib` assist in managing authentication effortlessly, helping you to focus on integrating functionality rather than getting bogged down in the complexities of security protocols.

Error handling is an important consideration when working with APIs. Network issues, server errors, and unexpected data formats can all lead to failed requests. Python's exception handling mechanisms, along with proper status code checks, can help you manage these situations gracefully. Learning to interpret the response codes returned by an API, such as 200 for success or 404 for not found, is essential for debugging and ensuring that your application behaves reliably. By incorporating robust error handling, you can build applications that are not only functional but also resilient to the various challenges posed by external services.

Finally, the versatility of APIs allows for their application across a multitude of domains. Whether you're developing a web application that integrates social media feeds, analyzing data from an external database, or building a machine learning model that pulls in datasets from various sources, APIs can significantly enhance the capabilities of your projects. By understanding how to work with APIs, Python developers can tap into vast resources and functionalities, paving the way for innovative solutions in fields such as data science, automation, and artificial intelligence. As you progress in your coding journey, mastering API interactions will undoubtedly empower you to create more dynamic and responsive applications.

Deploying Your Web Application

Deploying your web application is a crucial step in the development lifecycle, transforming your code from a local environment into a live product accessible to users. This process involves several key stages, including choosing a hosting provider, configuring your server, and managing your application's dependencies. Each of these components plays a significant role in ensuring that your application runs smoothly and can handle real-world user traffic.

One of the first decisions you'll need to make is selecting the right hosting provider. There are various options available, ranging from shared hosting to dedicated servers and cloud-based solutions. For beginners, platforms like Heroku, PythonAnywhere, and

DigitalOcean offer user-friendly interfaces and scalability options. If you're developing a data-driven web application, ensure that your selected provider can handle the necessary database management systems, such as PostgreSQL or MySQL, which are commonly used in Python web applications.

After choosing a hosting service, the next step is to configure your server environment. This includes setting up the operating system, installing required software packages, and configuring web servers like Nginx or Apache. It's essential to establish a secure environment, which involves configuring firewalls, applying necessary updates, and securing sensitive data. For Python applications, using a virtual environment can help manage dependencies and avoid conflicts between different projects. Tools like pip and virtualenv are invaluable for maintaining a clean workspace.

Once your server is configured, deploying your application involves transferring your code and assets to the server. This can be done using various methods, including Secure Copy Protocol (SCP), Git, or deployment automation tools like Fabric or Ansible. It's critical to ensure that your deployment process is consistent and repeatable to minimize downtime and errors. Continuous integration and deployment (CI/CD) practices can significantly enhance this process, allowing for automated testing and deployment each time you push code changes.

Finally, monitoring your deployed web application is vital for maintaining performance and reliability. Implementing logging and monitoring tools can help you track user interactions, identify errors, and optimize performance. Services like New Relic, Sentry, or even simple logging with Python's built-in logging module can provide insights into your application's behavior in a production environment. As your application scales, you'll also want to consider load balancing and redundancy strategies to handle increased traffic effectively, ensuring a seamless experience for users.

Chapter 4: Python for Machine Learning

Introduction to Machine Learning

Machine learning, a subset of artificial intelligence, has significantly transformed various industries by enabling computers to learn from data and improve their performance over time without being explicitly programmed. As coders and computer science students delve into the world of programming, understanding machine learning becomes essential. This introduction serves as a foundation for those interested in leveraging Python to develop machine learning applications, a skill increasingly sought after in the technology sector.

The core concept of machine learning revolves around algorithms that analyze and learn from data. These algorithms can identify patterns, make predictions, and provide insights based on the input data they receive. Python, with its simplicity and versatility, has emerged as a leading programming language for machine learning. Its extensive libraries, such as TensorFlow, Keras, and Scikit-learn, offer powerful tools that simplify the implementation of complex machine learning models, making it accessible for beginners and experienced developers alike.

There are three primary types of machine learning: supervised learning, unsupervised learning, and reinforcement learning. Supervised learning involves training a model on a labeled dataset, where the input data is paired with the correct output. Unsupervised learning, on the other hand, deals with unlabeled data, allowing the model to discover patterns and groupings on its own. Reinforcement learning focuses on training models to make decisions by rewarding them for desirable actions, often used in robotics and game development. Each type of learning has its applications and is suited for different tasks, providing a broad spectrum of opportunities for aspiring machine learning practitioners.

As the demand for data-driven decision-making continues to rise, proficiency in machine learning becomes a valuable asset. Whether working in data analysis, web development, or artificial intelligence, understanding how to implement machine learning algorithms can elevate the capabilities of projects and initiatives. For example, in data analysis, machine learning can enhance predictive analytics, while in web development, it can improve user experience through personalized recommendations.

In conclusion, machine learning represents a pivotal shift in how we interact with technology and data. By mastering the foundational concepts and tools available in Python, coders and computer science students can harness the power of machine learning to create innovative solutions across various domains. This journey not only enhances technical skills but also opens doors to exciting career opportunities in a rapidly evolving field.

Libraries for Machine Learning: Scikit-Learn and TensorFlow

Scikit-Learn and TensorFlow are two of the most popular libraries in Python for machine learning, each catering to different needs within the field. Scikit-Learn is primarily designed for traditional machine learning tasks, providing a user-friendly interface for building models using a variety of algorithms. It offers a straightforward approach to data preprocessing, model selection, and evaluation, making it an excellent choice for beginners in the field. With its extensive documentation and community support, Scikit-Learn allows developers to implement algorithms like regression, classification, clustering, and dimensionality reduction with ease.

On the other hand, TensorFlow is a more comprehensive framework that is particularly suited for deep learning applications. Developed by Google, TensorFlow provides a powerful platform for creating complex neural networks and handling large datasets. It offers a range of tools that allow users to build and train models efficiently, leveraging the computational power of CPUs and GPUs. The flexibility of TensorFlow means that it can be used for a wide variety of tasks, from image recognition to natural language processing, making it a go-to choice for advanced machine learning practitioners.

When starting with Scikit-Learn, users can quickly set up their environment and begin working with datasets.

The library supports various file formats, making data input and manipulation straightforward. Additionally, Scikit-Learn includes numerous built-in datasets for practice, allowing users to experiment with different algorithms without the need for extensive data collection. The library emphasizes modularity, enabling users to easily switch between different models and tune hyperparameters to optimize performance. This accessibility makes Scikit-Learn an ideal starting point for coders and computer science students looking to build their foundational skills in machine learning.

In contrast, TensorFlow's setup may appear more complex, given its extensive functionalities and capabilities. However, once the initial learning curve is overcome, users can take advantage of its advanced features, such as TensorBoard for visualization and Keras for high-level model building. These tools streamline the process of developing and refining deep learning models. TensorFlow's support for distributed computing also allows it to scale applications to handle larger datasets, catering to the needs of more experienced developers working on significant projects in artificial intelligence and data analysis.

Both Scikit-Learn and TensorFlow play essential roles in the machine learning ecosystem, and understanding their respective strengths will empower coders and technology enthusiasts to choose the right tool for their projects. Whether one is interested in straightforward model building or delving into the complexities of neural networks, these libraries provide robust frameworks for exploration and experimentation. As machine learning continues to evolve, familiarity with these tools will be invaluable for anyone looking to harness the power of data in various domains.

Supervised vs Unsupervised Learning

Supervised and unsupervised learning are two fundamental paradigms in machine learning, each serving distinct purposes and utilizing different methodologies. Supervised learning involves training a model on a labeled dataset, where the input data is paired with the corresponding correct output. This method allows the model to learn from examples, making predictions based on the relationships it identifies during training. Common applications of supervised learning include classification tasks, such as identifying whether an email is spam or not, and regression tasks, where the goal is to predict continuous values, such as forecasting stock prices.

In contrast, unsupervised learning deals with datasets that lack labeled responses. The goal of unsupervised learning is to find patterns or groupings within the data. This approach is particularly useful in exploratory data analysis, where understanding the inherent structure of the data can reveal insights that were not initially apparent. For instance, clustering algorithms can identify groups of similar customers based on their purchasing behavior, while dimensionality reduction techniques can simplify complex datasets by reducing the number of features while retaining essential information.

The choice between supervised and unsupervised learning often depends on the specific problem at hand and the availability of labeled data. If a sufficient amount of labeled training data is available, supervised learning is typically preferred due to its accuracy and ability to provide specific predictions. Conversely, when labeled data is scarce or when the goal is to explore the data without preconceived notions, unsupervised learning becomes the method of choice. It is essential to understand the characteristics of the dataset and the desired outcomes to select the appropriate learning strategy.

Both supervised and unsupervised learning can be implemented effectively using Python, a versatile programming language widely used in data analysis and machine learning. Libraries such as Scikit-learn provide robust tools for both types of learning, enabling coders and data scientists to easily apply algorithms, preprocess data, and evaluate model performance. With Python's rich ecosystem, users can efficiently handle various tasks, from building predictive models to uncovering patterns within datasets, making it an indispensable resource for those interested in machine learning.

In summary, supervised and unsupervised learning represent two distinct approaches to machine learning, each with its unique strengths and applications. Understanding the differences between these methods allows coders and computer science students to choose the right approach for their specific projects. As technology continues to evolve, the ability to leverage these learning paradigms will be critical for anyone looking to delve into the realms of data analysis, artificial intelligence, and beyond.

Building and Evaluating Models

Building and evaluating models is a critical aspect of many applications in Python, particularly in fields such as data analysis, machine learning, and artificial intelligence. The process typically begins with defining the problem you wish to solve, which might involve predicting outcomes, classifying data, or identifying patterns. Once the problem is clearly defined, the next step is to gather and preprocess the data. This includes cleaning the data to remove any inaccuracies, handling missing values, and transforming variables to ensure they are in a suitable format for modeling. Python libraries such as Pandas and NumPy are invaluable during this phase, allowing for efficient data manipulation and analysis.

After data preparation, the next step is to select an appropriate model. This choice depends on various factors, including the nature of the data, the problem type, and the desired outcome. For instance, if you're engaging in a supervised learning task, you might choose models like linear regression or decision trees, while unsupervised tasks could lead you toward clustering algorithms like K-means. Python offers a plethora of libraries, such as Scikit-learn, TensorFlow, and Keras, which provide a wide range of algorithms to cater to different modeling needs. Understanding the theoretical foundations behind these models is essential, as it enables you to make informed decisions about which algorithms to apply.

Once a model is selected, it must be trained using a portion of the available data—commonly referred to as the training set. This involves feeding the data into the model and allowing it to learn the underlying patterns. During this phase, it is crucial to monitor the model's performance using metrics relevant to the specific task, such as accuracy, precision, recall, or F1-score. Python's Scikit-learn library offers straightforward functions to compute these metrics, helping you assess your model's effectiveness during training.

Evaluation of the model is a vital step that follows training. This process typically involves testing the model on a separate dataset known as the test set, which was not used during the training phase. This step is crucial to ensure that the model generalizes well to unseen data. Common evaluation strategies include cross-validation, where the dataset is divided into multiple subsets to validate the model's performance iteratively. By comparing the model's predictions against the actual outcomes, you can identify areas for improvement and refine your approach, whether it involves tuning hyperparameters or selecting a different model altogether.

In conclusion, building and evaluating models in Python is a structured process that encompasses problem definition, data preparation, model selection, training, and evaluation. Mastering these steps equips coders, computer science students, and technology enthusiasts with the essential skills needed to tackle real-world problems across various domains, including web development, scientific computing, and cybersecurity. As you delve deeper into Python, leveraging its rich ecosystem of libraries will empower you to create robust models that can drive insights and innovation in your projects.

Practical Machine Learning Projects

Practical machine learning projects serve as a bridge between theoretical knowledge and real-world application. They offer coders and computer science students an opportunity to apply their skills in Python while exploring the fascinating world of machine learning. These projects often range from beginner-friendly tasks that help solidify foundational concepts to more advanced applications that challenge seasoned learners. By engaging in practical projects, individuals can enhance their understanding of algorithms, data processing, and model evaluation, all while building a portfolio that showcases their capabilities in Python.

One of the simplest yet impactful machine learning projects is developing a predictive model using a dataset. For instance, coders can utilize the widely accessible Iris dataset to classify different species of flowers based on their features. This project introduces fundamental machine learning concepts such as data preprocessing, feature engineering, and model selection. Using libraries like scikit-learn, learners can implement various algorithms, such as decision trees or support vector machines, to train their models and evaluate their performance. This hands-on experience is invaluable for grasping how machine learning operates and understanding the importance of data quality.

Another engaging project involves creating a recommendation system, which is a staple in web development and e-commerce. By leveraging collaborative filtering or content-based filtering techniques, students can build a system that suggests products or content based on user preferences. Implementing this project requires knowledge of data manipulation with pandas and the application of machine learning algorithms to generate recommendations. This project not only enhances Python skills but also offers insights into user behavior analysis and the practical implications of machine learning in enhancing user experiences.

For those interested in automation and scripting, developing a machine learning model for sentiment analysis presents a compelling challenge. By analyzing textual data from social media, product reviews, or news articles, coders can train a model to determine the sentiment expressed in the text. Using natural language processing libraries like NLTK or spaCy, learners can preprocess the data, extract features, and apply machine learning techniques to classify sentiments as positive, negative, or neutral. This project highlights the intersection of machine learning and text analysis, showing how Python can be utilized to automate the understanding of large volumes of unstructured data.

Finally, integrating machine learning into IoT applications offers an exciting frontier for coders and tech enthusiasts. A practical project could involve analyzing sensor data from IoT devices to predict equipment failures or optimize energy consumption. By using Python libraries such as TensorFlow or Keras, learners can develop models that learn from real-time data, enabling proactive maintenance or resource management. This project not only illustrates the versatility of machine learning but also prepares students for future trends in automation and smart technology, reinforcing the relevance of Python in modern computing landscapes.

Chapter 5: Python for Automation and Scripting

What is Automation?

Automation refers to the use of technology to perform tasks with minimal human intervention. In the context of programming and coding, automation allows for the execution of repetitive tasks efficiently and accurately, freeing up time for more complex problem-solving. With the advent of powerful programming languages like Python, automation has become increasingly accessible to coders and computer science students alike. This capability not only enhances productivity but also allows for the creation of more sophisticated applications across various domains, including data analysis, web development, and machine learning.

One of the primary benefits of automation is its ability to increase efficiency. In many industries, processes that were once manual and time-consuming can now be streamlined through scripts and tools. For instance, in data analysis, Python can be used to automate data collection, cleansing, and visualization, leading to quicker insights and decision-making. Similarly, in web development, automation can handle tasks such as testing, deployment, and even routine updates, thereby reducing human error and ensuring consistency across projects.

Automation is particularly valuable in the realm of machine learning and artificial intelligence. Here, Python scripts can automate the data preprocessing stages, model training, and evaluation processes, allowing data scientists to focus on refining algorithms and interpreting results rather than getting bogged down by repetitive tasks. This not only accelerates the development cycle but also encourages experimentation and innovation, as coders can quickly iterate on their models without the overhead of manual intervention.

In addition to enhancing efficiency in specific fields, automation has significant implications for the Internet of Things (IoT) and scientific computing. For IoT applications, automation enables devices to communicate and respond to conditions in real-time, making systems smarter and more responsive. In scientific computing, automation can facilitate complex simulations and computations, allowing researchers to tackle large-scale problems that would be impractical to solve manually. Python's extensive libraries and frameworks support these automation tasks, making it an ideal choice for professionals in these areas.

Ultimately, automation represents a paradigm shift in how tasks are approached in coding and technology. By leveraging Python's capabilities, coders and computer science students can harness automation to not only simplify their workflows but also to drive innovation and efficiency in their projects. As technology continues to evolve, understanding and implementing automation will be crucial for anyone looking to stay relevant in the fast-paced world of coding and development.

Writing Scripts for Automation

Writing scripts for automation is an essential skill for anyone looking to optimize workflows and increase efficiency in various tasks. Automation scripts can be utilized in numerous domains, from data analysis to web development, and even in machine learning projects. By leveraging Python, a versatile and powerful programming language, coders and computer science students can create scripts that automate repetitive tasks, enabling them to focus on more complex problems. Understanding the fundamentals of automation scripting in Python not only enhances productivity but also cultivates a deeper appreciation for coding as a means to solve real-world challenges.

To begin writing automation scripts, it is crucial to understand the core principles of scripting in Python. Python's simple syntax and extensive standard library make it an ideal language for beginners and experienced developers alike. Familiarity with concepts such as control flow, data types, functions, and modules is vital. By mastering these foundational elements, coders can construct scripts that efficiently handle various tasks, such as file management, data processing, and web scraping. Furthermore, Python's support for libraries like os, shutil, and requests provides additional tools to streamline automation processes.

One of the most common applications of automation scripting is in the realm of data analysis. With the rise of big data, professionals are often tasked with processing large datasets that require repetitive operations. Python's pandas library is particularly useful for automating data manipulation tasks, allowing users to read, clean, and analyze data with minimal effort. By writing scripts that automate these processes, students and tech enthusiasts can save time and reduce the likelihood of human error, ultimately leading to more accurate analyses and informed decision-making.

In the context of web development, automation scripts can significantly enhance the efficiency of tasks such as deployment, testing, and monitoring. Tools like Flask and Django can be integrated with automation scripts to streamline the development workflow. For instance, writing scripts that automate the deployment of web applications can simplify the process of updating code and managing server configurations. Moreover, automation can be employed to run tests automatically, ensuring that code changes do not introduce new bugs and that applications continue to function correctly after updates.

Finally, as technology evolves, the importance of automation scripts in fields like machine learning, IoT, and cybersecurity cannot be overstated. In machine learning, automation can facilitate the training and evaluation of models, allowing developers to experiment with different algorithms and parameters without manual intervention. In the realm of IoT, automation scripts can manage the communication between devices, ensuring seamless operation in smart environments. Similarly, in cybersecurity, automation can help monitor systems for vulnerabilities and respond to threats more quickly. As coders and technology enthusiasts continue to explore these niches, mastering the art of writing automation scripts in Python will undoubtedly be a valuable asset in their toolkit.

Working with Files and Directories

Working with files and directories is a fundamental aspect of programming in Python that enables developers to manage data efficiently. Python provides a rich set of built-in libraries to handle file operations, making it straightforward to read from and write to files. The most commonly used library for file handling is the built-in `open()` function, which allows programmers to access files in various modes, such as read ('r'), write ('w'), append ('a'), and more. Understanding how to open, read, write, and close files is essential for tasks ranging from data analysis to automation and scripting.

When working with directories, Python's `os` module is an invaluable tool. It provides functions to create, remove, and change directories, as well as to list files within a directory. For example, `os.listdir()` can be used to retrieve a list of all the files in a specified directory, which is particularly useful for automation scripts that need to process multiple files. Additionally, the `os.path` submodule offers functions to manipulate file paths, allowing developers to construct or deconstruct paths in a platform-independent manner. This is crucial when developing applications intended to run across different operating systems.

File handling in Python is not limited to basic operations. The `shutil` module extends functionality by allowing users to copy, move, and delete files and directories with ease. This can be particularly beneficial in data analysis and machine learning projects, where large datasets may need to be rearranged or cleaned up regularly. For instance, moving files from a raw data directory to a processed data directory can be automated using `shutil.move()`, thereby streamlining the workflow and reducing manual intervention.

Error handling is another essential aspect when working with files and directories. Python provides mechanisms such as try-except blocks to manage exceptions that may arise during file operations, such as file not found errors or permission issues. By implementing robust error handling, developers can create scripts that fail gracefully, providing informative feedback to the user. This is especially important in environments like web development and automation, where unexpected errors can disrupt user experience or lead to data loss.

In summary, mastering file and directory operations in Python is critical for a wide range of applications, from simple scripts to complex data processing tasks. By leveraging the built-in capabilities of Python's standard libraries, programmers can efficiently manage their data and resources. Familiarity with these concepts not only enhances coding skills but also serves as a foundation for more advanced programming challenges in fields such as data analysis, web development, and machine learning. As you progress in your coding journey, these skills will prove invaluable in handling real-world problems effectively.

Automating Web Scraping

Automating web scraping is a powerful technique that allows programmers to extract data from websites efficiently. In the realm of Python, various libraries facilitate this process, making it accessible even to those with minimal coding experience. The primary goal of web scraping is to gather useful information from the internet, which can then be analyzed, visualized, or used in applications. This subchapter will explore how to automate web scraping using Python, focusing on essential libraries, best practices, and real-world applications.

The most commonly used library for web scraping in Python is Beautiful Soup. This library provides tools for parsing HTML and XML documents, allowing users to navigate and search through the parse tree easily. Combined with requests, another Python library that allows you to send HTTP requests, Beautiful Soup becomes a potent tool for downloading and processing web pages. By automating the retrieval of web content, coders can set up scripts that run at specified intervals, ensuring they always have the latest data without manual intervention.

Another significant library in the Python ecosystem for web scraping is Scrapy. Unlike Beautiful Soup, which is primarily focused on parsing, Scrapy is a full-fledged web scraping framework that allows users to build complex scrapers. It supports asynchronous processing, which means it can handle multiple requests simultaneously, leading to faster data collection. Scrapy also includes features like built-in support for handling cookies, user agents, and even exporting data in various formats such as JSON or CSV. This makes it suitable for more extensive and complicated scraping tasks.

To automate web scraping effectively, it is crucial to adhere to ethical guidelines and legal considerations. Many websites have terms of service that explicitly prohibit scraping, and violating these can lead to being banned from the site or facing legal repercussions. It is essential to respect the robots.txt file of a website, which indicates which parts of the site can be accessed by automated agents. Additionally, implementing delays between requests can help avoid overwhelming servers and reduce the risk of being detected as a bot, ensuring a more sustainable scraping approach.

The applications of automated web scraping are vast and varied. In data analysis, for example, marketers can scrape competitor prices or trends to inform their strategies. Researchers might collect data for studies or surveys, while developers can gather information to enhance their applications. Furthermore, in the realm of machine learning, scraped data can serve as training datasets for algorithms. By automating the scraping process, coders streamline their workflows, allowing them to focus on analyzing and deriving insights from the data rather than spending time collecting it manually.

Practical Automation Projects

Practical automation projects serve as an excellent entry point for coders and computer science students looking to harness the power of Python. Automation is increasingly becoming a vital skill across various domains such as data analysis, web development, and even machine learning. By engaging in hands-on projects, beginners can solidify their understanding of Python's capabilities while also producing tangible outcomes that can be utilized in real-world scenarios. This subchapter will explore a variety of practical automation projects tailored to enhance coding skills across multiple niches.

One popular automation project is creating a web scraper. Web scraping involves extracting data from websites, which can be particularly useful for data analysis and research purposes. Using libraries such as Beautiful Soup and Requests, a beginner can build a script that retrieves and organizes data into a structured format. This project not only showcases Python's web interaction capabilities but also emphasizes the importance of ethical scraping practices, ensuring that users respect website terms of service and privacy considerations.

Another engaging project is automating file organization on a computer. By writing a Python script that sorts files into designated folders based on their file types, users can streamline their workflow and maintain a tidy digital workspace. This project introduces essential programming concepts such as file handling, conditional statements, and loops. Furthermore, it empowers users to customize their automation scripts according to specific needs, making it a versatile tool for personal or professional use.

In the realm of machine learning, automating the data preprocessing phase can significantly enhance efficiency. A beginner can create a script that automates tasks such as data cleaning, normalization, and encoding of categorical variables. This project not only fosters a deeper understanding of data manipulation libraries like Pandas and NumPy but also illustrates the critical role of preprocessing in the machine learning pipeline. By automating this process, coders can focus more on model development and testing, thus accelerating their learning journey in artificial intelligence.

For those interested in the Internet of Things (IoT), automating home devices through Python can be both fun and educational. By utilizing libraries like Flask for web development and Raspberry Pi for hardware integration, beginners can create a simple home automation system. This project might involve controlling lights, fans, or even security cameras remotely via a web interface. Not only does this project allow coders to explore the intersection of software and hardware, but it also provides a practical demonstration of how Python can be used to enhance everyday living.

Ultimately, practical automation projects are invaluable for coders and technology enthusiasts. They not only reinforce Python programming skills but also provide opportunities to explore various fields such as data analysis, web development, and IoT. Each project is a stepping stone towards mastering Python, allowing beginners to learn through experimentation and creativity. By engaging in these projects, learners can build a robust portfolio that showcases their skills and prepares them for future challenges in the ever-evolving tech landscape.

Chapter 6: Python for Game Development

Overview of Game Development

Game development is a multifaceted process that combines creativity, technology, and a keen understanding of user experience. At its core, the development of a game involves several stages: concept creation, design, programming, testing, and deployment. Each stage requires a unique set of skills and knowledge, making game development both a collaborative and interdisciplinary endeavor. With the rise of accessible programming languages like Python, aspiring developers can dive into game creation with relative ease, harnessing its simplicity and versatility to bring their ideas to life.

The initial phase of game development typically begins with brainstorming ideas and creating a game concept. This involves defining the game's genre, target audience, and core mechanics. Designers create storyboards and sketches to visualize the game world, characters, and user interfaces. While this phase is heavily focused on creativity, technical considerations such as platform compatibility and performance constraints also play a crucial role. Python's rich libraries and frameworks, such as Pygame, offer developers the tools necessary to prototype their ideas and iterate quickly.

Once the concept is solidified, the development phase begins. This is where programming comes into play, and Python shines as a language for both beginners and experienced developers. Its readability and extensive libraries facilitate the implementation of game logic, physics, graphics, and sound. Developers can utilize existing frameworks to handle complex tasks like collision detection and rendering, allowing them to focus on the unique aspects of their game. Additionally, Python's support for object-oriented programming encourages developers to create reusable code, enhancing efficiency and maintainability.

Testing is a critical stage in game development, ensuring that the game functions as intended and provides a smooth user experience. This phase often involves rigorous playtesting, where developers gather feedback and identify bugs or design flaws. Python's ease of use allows for rapid iteration and debugging, enabling developers to refine their games based on real user interactions. Automated testing tools can also be integrated into the development process, further streamlining quality assurance and improving the final product's reliability.

Finally, deployment and marketing are essential for bringing a game to its audience. This includes choosing the right distribution platforms, such as Steam or mobile app stores, and executing marketing strategies to attract players. Python's versatility extends to web development as well, allowing developers to create promotional websites or online communities to engage with their players. The game development landscape is continually evolving, and by leveraging Python's capabilities, new developers can enter this exciting field with the confidence to create innovative and engaging gaming experiences.

Introduction to Pygame

Pygame is a popular library in Python that simplifies the process of creating games and multimedia applications. It serves as an ideal platform for beginners eager to dive into game development while leveraging their existing knowledge of Python. Pygame provides a rich set of modules to handle graphics, sounds, and user input, making it an attractive choice for those who want to combine their coding skills with creativity. Its simplicity allows developers to focus more on game design and mechanics rather than getting bogged down by complex programming concepts.

Developed in 2000, Pygame has evolved significantly, supported by a vibrant community that contributes to its development and documentation. The library is built on top of the Simple DirectMedia Layer (SDL), which is a cross-platform development library used for writing games and multimedia applications. This foundational layer ensures that Pygame can run on multiple operating systems, including Windows, macOS, and Linux, thus broadening its accessibility. The community-driven aspect of Pygame ensures that newcomers can find ample resources, tutorials, and forums to aid their learning process.

One of the standout features of Pygame is its ease of use. With straightforward functions and a well-structured API, developers can quickly set up a game window, draw shapes, and respond to user inputs. This user-friendly nature is particularly beneficial for those who may have experience in other Python niches but are new to game development. Additionally, Pygame supports various media formats, allowing developers to incorporate images, sounds, and music seamlessly. This capability enhances the overall gaming experience and encourages experimentation with different media.

Pygame is not only suitable for creating traditional games; it also serves as an excellent educational tool. Many computer science educators utilize Pygame in their curricula to teach programming concepts and software development principles. Students can learn about game loops, event handling, and collision detection while actively engaging in a project that is both fun and rewarding. This hands-on experience can reinforce theoretical knowledge, making it easier for learners to grasp complex programming ideas.

In recent years, Pygame has seen renewed interest as game development has become more mainstream. Whether you're a coder looking to design your first game, a computer science student seeking practical applications of your studies, or a technology enthusiast eager to explore the world of interactive media, Pygame offers an accessible entry point. As you embark on your journey with Pygame, you will not only enhance your programming skills but also tap into a creative outlet that can lead to exciting projects and collaborations within the tech community.

Designing Game Mechanics

Designing game mechanics is a crucial aspect of game development that can significantly influence the player experience and overall engagement. Game mechanics are the rules and systems that govern how a game operates, including player actions, objectives, and interactions with the game world. When designing these mechanics, it is essential to consider the target audience, the intended gameplay experience, and the story you want to tell through your game. This foundational understanding helps ensure that the mechanics align with the overall vision of the game, creating a cohesive and enjoyable experience for players.

In Python, creating game mechanics involves utilizing libraries such as Pygame, which provides tools for game development, allowing coders to focus on designing engaging gameplay instead of getting lost in low-level programming details. Pygame helps manage graphics, sound, and user input, enabling developers to prototype and iterate on game mechanics quickly. For example, implementing a simple scoring system can be done by defining variables to track player scores and updating these variables based on in-game actions. This simplicity encourages experimentation, which is vital when refining mechanics to enhance player engagement and satisfaction.

A well-designed game mechanic must also cater to different player skill levels. This can be achieved by incorporating elements such as difficulty scaling, where gameplay becomes more challenging as players progress. For instance, a mechanic that adjusts enemy strength based on the player's performance can maintain a balance that keeps players invested. Additionally, incorporating tutorials or guidance for new players can help bridge the gap for beginners, ensuring they understand the mechanics without feeling overwhelmed. This thoughtful approach to design can lead to a more inclusive gaming experience, appealing to a broader audience.

Another essential aspect of designing game mechanics is ensuring they promote player agency and decision-making. Players should feel that their choices have meaningful consequences, which can be accomplished by designing branching paths or multiple endings based on player actions. In Python, this can be achieved through the use of conditionals and state management, allowing the game to respond dynamically to players' decisions. By fostering a sense of ownership over their gameplay experience, developers can create a more immersive environment that encourages players to explore and engage deeply with the game.

Finally, playtesting is an indispensable part of the game mechanics design process. Gathering feedback from actual players can highlight areas where mechanics may fall short or become frustrating. By iterating on these mechanics based on player input, developers can refine their designs to enhance enjoyment and engagement. Python’s versatility allows for rapid prototyping of game mechanics, making it easier to implement changes and test new ideas. This iterative cycle of design, testing, and refinement is crucial in crafting compelling game mechanics that resonate with players and elevate their gaming experience.

Creating Graphics and Sounds

Creating graphics and sounds in Python is a crucial aspect for those venturing into game development, multimedia applications, or any project requiring visual and auditory elements. Python offers several libraries that simplify the process of integrating graphics and sounds into your applications. The most popular library for handling graphics is Pygame, which provides a robust framework for creating games and multimedia applications. Pygame enables you to manage images, animations, and sounds with ease, making it ideal for both beginners and advanced coders.

To begin utilizing Pygame, you first need to install the library. This is typically done via pip, Python's package installer. Once installed, you can start creating a window for your application where all graphics will be displayed. Pygame provides functions to set up the display, manage the event loop, and update the screen. You can load images in various formats, draw shapes, and create animations by updating the positions of images over time. This allows you to create dynamic visuals that enhance user interaction and experience.

In addition to graphics, sound integration is another critical component of engaging applications. Pygame supports sound and music playback through its mixer module. By loading sound files and controlling playback, you can add background music, sound effects, and other audio elements to your project. This not only enriches the user experience but also helps in building an immersive environment, especially in gaming scenarios. Understanding how to manage audio playback, including volume control and sound looping, is essential for creating polished applications.

For those interested in more advanced graphics, the use of libraries like Matplotlib or Seaborn can be explored for data visualization purposes. These libraries allow you to create graphs, charts, and other visual representations of data, making them particularly useful in data analysis and scientific computing. By combining these visualizations with sound elements, you can create interactive dashboards or educational tools that provide both auditory and visual feedback to the user.

Ultimately, creating graphics and sounds in Python is about enhancing the interactivity and appeal of your projects. Whether you are developing a simple game, a data visualization tool, or a multimedia application, mastering these elements will elevate your coding skills and expand the potential of your projects. As you delve deeper into Python's capabilities, the integration of graphics and sounds will open new avenues for creativity and innovation in your coding journey.

Building a Simple Game

Building a simple game is an engaging way to apply your Python programming skills and deepen your understanding of the language. This subchapter will guide you through the process of creating a basic text-based game, which can serve as a foundation for more complex projects in the future. By utilizing fundamental programming concepts such as variables, control flow, and functions, you will not only enjoy the creative aspect of game development but also reinforce your coding knowledge.

To start, we will create a simple guessing game where the player has to guess a number within a certain range. First, you'll need to import the random library, which will allow us to generate random numbers. With this library, we can create a function that selects a number between 1 and 100. The player will then be prompted to guess the number, and we will provide feedback based on their input, indicating whether their guess is too high, too low, or correct. This interaction will introduce you to user input handling and basic conditional statements.

Next, we can enhance the game by adding a scoring system. Players will have a limited number of attempts to guess the correct number, which will make the game more challenging and exciting. You can implement a variable to keep track of the number of attempts remaining and another variable to count the score based on how quickly the player guesses the number. This addition will require you to practice loops and condition checks, reinforcing your understanding of game mechanics and how to manage game states.

After establishing the core mechanics, consider introducing additional features to make the game more engaging. For instance, you could add difficulty levels that change the range of numbers or the number of allowed guesses. You might also implement a restart option that allows players to play multiple rounds without restarting the program. These enhancements will not only make the game more enjoyable but also provide opportunities to practice more advanced programming concepts, such as functions and modular design.

Finally, once your game is functioning, think about how you can share it with others. You can package your game as a standalone script, share it on platforms like GitHub, or even create a simple web interface using Python's Flask framework for a more interactive experience. This step will introduce you to collaboration, version control, and deployment, which are essential skills in the coding world. By building this simple game, you will not only gain practical programming experience but also lay the groundwork for exploring more advanced game development projects in Python.

Chapter 7: Python for Artificial Intelligence

Understanding Artificial Intelligence

Artificial Intelligence (AI) has emerged as one of the most transformative technologies of our time, influencing various fields and applications across the globe. At its core, AI refers to the capability of a machine to imitate intelligent human behavior. This encompasses a range of technologies, including machine learning, natural language processing, computer vision, and robotics. Understanding AI is crucial for coders and computer science students, as it opens up a plethora of opportunities in developing smarter applications and systems. By leveraging languages like Python, individuals can dive into the world of AI, making it accessible and manageable for those just beginning their coding journey.

Machine learning, a subset of AI, enables systems to learn from data and improve over time without explicit programming. This approach is particularly relevant for Python developers, as the language boasts powerful libraries such as TensorFlow, Keras, and scikit-learn. These tools simplify the process of building, training, and deploying machine learning models, making it easier for coders to incorporate AI capabilities into their projects. Whether it's for data analysis, web development, or automation, understanding how machine learning functions allows developers to create applications that can predict outcomes, recognize patterns, and even make decisions based on data inputs.

Natural language processing (NLP) is another vital area of AI that focuses on the interaction between computers and humans through natural language. As technology progresses, the ability for machines to understand and interpret human language is becoming increasingly sophisticated. Python offers numerous libraries, such as NLTK and SpaCy, that facilitate NLP tasks, allowing coders to develop chatbots, sentiment analysis tools, and language translation applications. By grasping the fundamentals of NLP, developers can enhance user experiences and create more engaging applications that resonate with users on a personal level.

Computer vision, which enables machines to interpret and make decisions based on visual data, plays a significant role in various applications, from security systems to autonomous vehicles. Python's libraries like OpenCV and PIL provide robust tools for image processing and analysis. Understanding how computer vision works allows developers to integrate visual data into their applications, which can lead to innovative solutions in fields such as robotics, healthcare, and gaming. By mastering the concepts of computer vision, coders can push the boundaries of what their applications can achieve.

Lastly, the ethical considerations surrounding AI are an essential aspect of understanding this technology. As AI systems become more prevalent, the potential for bias and misuse raises critical questions about accountability, transparency, and fairness. Coders and computer science students must be aware of these issues to build responsible and equitable AI systems. By fostering a strong ethical framework, developers can ensure that their work contributes positively to society, paving the way for a future where technology enhances human capabilities while addressing the challenges that arise from its implementation.

Libraries for AI: TensorFlow and Keras

In the landscape of artificial intelligence and machine learning, TensorFlow and Keras have emerged as two of the most powerful and widely used libraries in Python. Developed by Google, TensorFlow provides a robust framework for building machine learning models, while Keras, which can be thought of as a high-level API for TensorFlow, simplifies the process of creating and training neural networks. Together, they enable coders, computer science students, and technology enthusiasts to delve into the complexities of AI with relative ease. By leveraging these libraries, developers can focus more on model architecture and experimentation rather than getting bogged down in the intricacies of low-level programming.

TensorFlow is designed to handle large-scale machine learning tasks and is particularly well-suited for deep learning applications. It offers a flexible architecture that allows users to deploy computation across various platforms, whether on a single machine or across multiple devices in the cloud. The library supports a range of neural network architectures, including convolutional neural networks (CNNs) and recurrent neural networks (RNNs), which are essential for tasks such as image recognition and natural language processing. This versatility makes TensorFlow an ideal choice for anyone looking to implement advanced AI solutions.

Keras complements TensorFlow by providing a user-friendly interface that streamlines the process of building neural networks. With its modular approach, Keras allows developers to easily construct and modify models through simple code, promoting rapid experimentation and prototyping. The library abstracts many of the complexities involved in deep learning, making it accessible for beginners while still offering the flexibility that experienced developers need. By using Keras, coders can quickly set up and train models, enabling them to focus on fine-tuning their algorithms rather than wrestling with intricate details.

The integration of Keras with TensorFlow has led to a powerful synergy that enhances the capabilities of both libraries. Users can take advantage of Keras's simplicity while still tapping into TensorFlow's performance optimizations and scalability. This combination is particularly beneficial for machine learning projects that require both speed and efficiency. Furthermore, TensorFlow's comprehensive ecosystem includes tools for model deployment, data processing, and visualization, which helps streamline the entire machine learning workflow.

As the demand for AI solutions continues to grow across various sectors, mastering TensorFlow and Keras becomes increasingly valuable for those involved in technology. Whether you are interested in data analysis, automation, game development, or IoT applications, understanding these libraries can significantly enhance your skill set. By exploring TensorFlow and Keras, coders and computer science students can unlock the potential of machine learning and contribute to the evolving field of artificial intelligence, making impactful advancements in their respective areas of expertise.

Neural Networks and Deep Learning

Neural networks are a cornerstone of modern artificial intelligence, mimicking the way the human brain processes information. At their core, neural networks consist of interconnected layers of nodes, or "neurons," which work together to perform complex calculations. Each neuron receives input data, applies a mathematical transformation, and passes its output to the next layer. This structure allows neural networks to learn from data by adjusting the weights of the connections between neurons based on the errors of their predictions. As coders and computer science students delve into Python, understanding how to implement and work with neural networks opens up a world of possibilities in various fields, including machine learning and artificial intelligence.

Deep learning is a subset of machine learning that utilizes neural networks with many layers, hence the term "deep." These deep neural networks excel at capturing intricate patterns in large datasets, making them particularly effective for tasks such as image and speech recognition, natural language processing, and even game development. With the rise of big data, the ability of deep learning models to process vast amounts of information has made them increasingly popular. Python, with its rich ecosystem of libraries like TensorFlow and Keras, provides an accessible platform for beginners to experiment with deep learning techniques and develop powerful applications.

To build a neural network in Python, one typically starts by defining the architecture, which includes specifying the number of layers and the number of neurons in each layer. The choice of activation function, which determines how the output of each neuron is computed, is also crucial. Common activation functions include ReLU (Rectified Linear Unit), sigmoid, and softmax. After defining the architecture, the next step is to compile the model, specifying the optimizer and loss function. This is where coders can leverage Python's simplicity and readability to construct and modify their neural network models efficiently.

Training a neural network involves feeding it a dataset and allowing it to learn from the data by adjusting the weights through a process called backpropagation. This involves calculating the gradient of the loss function with respect to the weights and updating the weights in the direction that minimizes the loss. In Python, libraries like TensorFlow and PyTorch streamline this process, allowing developers to focus on the model's design and experimentation rather than the underlying mathematics. Additionally, these libraries provide tools for monitoring the training process, tuning hyperparameters, and evaluating model performance.

As the field of artificial intelligence continues to evolve, the importance of neural networks and deep learning cannot be overstated. For coders and computer science students, mastering these concepts in Python not only enhances their skill set but also positions them at the forefront of technological innovation. Whether it is for developing intelligent applications, automating tasks, or analyzing complex datasets, knowledge of neural networks and deep learning is indispensable. With continuous advancements in the field, the potential applications are boundless, making it an exciting area for exploration and growth.

Natural Language Processing with Python

Natural Language Processing (NLP) is a fascinating area of artificial intelligence that focuses on the interaction between computers and human language. With Python's extensive libraries and frameworks, working with NLP has become more accessible than ever. This subchapter will introduce readers to the fundamental concepts of NLP, the essential libraries available in Python, and practical applications that illustrate how to implement these techniques in various domains, including data analysis and machine learning.

One of the most popular libraries for NLP in Python is Natural Language Toolkit (NLTK). NLTK provides a comprehensive suite of tools for text processing, including tokenization, stemming, and lemmatization. It also offers resources such as corpora and lexical resources to facilitate linguistic analysis. Another powerful library is SpaCy, designed for efficiency and ease of use in production settings. SpaCy offers pre-trained models for various languages and capabilities such as named entity recognition and part-of-speech tagging, making it an excellent choice for developers who require robust NLP solutions.

Text preprocessing is a critical step in NLP to ensure that the data is clean and structured for analysis. This process often involves converting text to lowercase, removing punctuation, and eliminating stop words—common words that usually do not contribute significant meaning to the text. After preprocessing, techniques such as vectorization transform the text into numerical formats that machine learning algorithms can understand. Libraries like Scikit-learn provide tools for vectorization, enabling users to convert text data into feature vectors suitable for modeling.

Applications of NLP are vast and span multiple industries. In data analysis, NLP can be used for sentiment analysis, allowing organizations to gauge public opinion on products or services by analyzing social media posts and reviews. In web development, chatbots powered by NLP can enhance user experience by providing instant responses to customer inquiries. Furthermore, in the realm of machine learning, NLP techniques are pivotal for tasks such as document classification, summarization, and translation, showcasing the versatility of Python in handling complex language-based challenges.

As technology continues to evolve, the relevance of NLP in various fields will only grow. Python's role as a leading programming language for NLP ensures that coders, computer science students, and technology enthusiasts can harness its capabilities for innovative solutions. By mastering NLP with Python, learners open doors to exciting career opportunities in artificial intelligence, data science, and beyond, making it a crucial skill set in today's digital landscape.

AI Projects and Applications

AI projects and applications have become increasingly significant in various sectors, driven by the need for automation, data analysis, and enhanced decision-making processes. Python, as a versatile and powerful programming language, has emerged as a primary tool for developing AI solutions. Its simplicity and readability make it an ideal choice for beginners and experienced developers alike. From web development and game design to machine learning and IoT, Python is at the forefront of numerous projects that leverage artificial intelligence.

In the realm of machine learning, Python libraries such as TensorFlow, Keras, and Scikit-learn enable developers to build sophisticated models that can learn from and make predictions based on data. For instance, a common project might involve creating a predictive model for stock prices using historical data. By employing Python, coders can preprocess data, train machine learning algorithms, and evaluate their performance all within a cohesive environment. This ease of use encourages experimentation and innovation, allowing students and enthusiasts to tackle increasingly complex problems.

In web development, AI applications can enhance user experience and optimize operations. Python frameworks like Flask and Django integrate AI capabilities to provide personalized recommendations, automate customer support through chatbots, and analyze user behavior to refine marketing strategies. A typical project might involve building a recommendation system for an e-commerce site, where data on user preferences and purchasing history is analyzed to suggest relevant products. This not only improves customer satisfaction but also boosts sales, showcasing the practical impact of AI in commerce.

Automation and scripting are other areas where Python excels, particularly in tasks that require repetitive data handling or system monitoring. By utilizing libraries such as Selenium for web automation or Beautiful Soup for web scraping, developers can create scripts that automatically gather, analyze, and report on data without human intervention. For example, a project could involve developing a script that monitors social media platforms for brand mentions and compiles sentiment analysis reports, providing companies with valuable insights into public perception.

Finally, in scientific computing and cybersecurity, Python plays a crucial role in analyzing vast datasets and securing information systems. Projects in these domains often involve complex simulations, data modeling, or threat detection algorithms. For instance, a scientific computing project might utilize Python to analyze climate data, enabling researchers to predict weather patterns and assess environmental changes. In cybersecurity, Python scripts can be developed to identify vulnerabilities or automate penetration testing, highlighting its importance in safeguarding sensitive information. Through these diverse applications, Python proves to be an indispensable tool for coders and technology enthusiasts aiming to harness the power of artificial intelligence.

Chapter 8: Python for Internet of Things (IoT)

Introduction to IoT

The Internet of Things (IoT) represents a transformative shift in the way we interact with the physical world. By connecting everyday objects to the internet, IoT allows for the seamless exchange of data between devices, enabling automation and smarter decision-making processes. This interconnectedness is made possible through the integration of sensors, software, and other technologies. As a result, various sectors including healthcare, agriculture, transportation, and home automation are experiencing significant advancements, driven by the ability to collect and analyze real-time data.

At its core, IoT consists of devices equipped with sensors and actuators that communicate over the internet. These devices can be as simple as a temperature sensor in a smart thermostat or as complex as a fully autonomous vehicle. The data collected from these devices can be processed and analyzed to provide insights and improve efficiency. For instance, smart agriculture solutions enable farmers to monitor soil conditions and crop health, leading to more informed decisions about irrigation and fertilization. This data-driven approach is not only beneficial for individual users but also contributes to broader societal benefits, such as reducing resource consumption and minimizing waste.

Python has emerged as a leading programming language for IoT development due to its simplicity and versatility. With an extensive range of libraries and frameworks, Python allows developers to quickly prototype and deploy IoT solutions. Libraries such as MicroPython and CircuitPython are specifically tailored for microcontrollers, making it easier to interface with sensors and actuators. This accessibility encourages coders and computer science students to experiment with IoT projects, fostering innovation and creativity in the field.

Moreover, the integration of Python in IoT opens up opportunities for data analysis and machine learning. As IoT devices generate massive amounts of data, the ability to analyze this data effectively becomes crucial. Python's robust ecosystem for data analysis, including libraries like Pandas and NumPy, enables developers to extract valuable insights from the data collected by IoT devices. Additionally, machine learning frameworks such as TensorFlow and scikit-learn can be employed to create predictive models, enhancing the intelligence of IoT systems.

In summary, the Internet of Things is a rapidly evolving domain that intertwines technology with everyday life. For coders and technology enthusiasts, understanding the fundamentals of IoT and its applications is essential. With Python as a powerful tool in this journey, individuals can delve into the world of IoT, exploring its potential to innovate and reshape industries. Embracing IoT development not only enhances technical skills but also positions aspiring developers at the forefront of a technological revolution that is changing how we live and work.

Setting Up Raspberry Pi with Python

Setting up a Raspberry Pi with Python is an exciting way to immerse yourself in the world of coding while exploring the capabilities of this versatile microcomputer. The Raspberry Pi is a small, affordable device that can serve as a platform for various projects, from simple scripts to complex applications. To get started, you will need to gather a few essential components, including a Raspberry Pi board, a microSD card, a power supply, and peripherals such as a monitor, keyboard, and mouse. Once you have these items, you can begin the process of installing an operating system and setting up your programming environment.

The most common operating system for Raspberry Pi is Raspberry Pi OS, which is based on Debian Linux. You can download the latest version from the official Raspberry Pi website. To install the OS, you will first need to prepare your microSD card using a tool like Raspberry Pi Imager or balenaEtcher. After flashing the OS image onto the card, insert it into the Raspberry Pi, connect your peripherals, and power it up. The initial setup will guide you through configuring your system, including setting up Wi-Fi and creating a user account.

Once you complete the setup, you will have a fully functional Raspberry Pi ready for programming.

With the operating system in place, the next step is to install Python. Raspberry Pi OS comes with Python pre-installed, but it is essential to ensure you have the latest version. You can check your Python version by opening the terminal and typing "python3 --version." If you need to update, you can use the package manager apt-get to install the latest version. Additionally, you may want to install some useful libraries such as NumPy for data analysis, Flask for web development, or Pygame for game development, depending on your interests. This flexibility allows you to tailor your Raspberry Pi environment to your specific projects and learning goals.

Once Python is set up, you can start writing your first program. Open the Thonny IDE, which comes pre-installed with Raspberry Pi OS, and create a new file. A simple "Hello, World!" program is a great starting point to familiarize yourself with the coding environment. As you progress, you can explore more complex scripts that interact with the Raspberry Pi's GPIO pins to control hardware components like LEDs, motors, or sensors. This hands-on approach not only reinforces your coding skills but also provides tangible results that demonstrate the power of Python in the context of physical computing and the Internet of Things.

In conclusion, setting up a Raspberry Pi with Python opens a world of possibilities for aspiring coders and technology enthusiasts. Whether you are interested in data analysis, web development, or automation, the Raspberry Pi serves as an excellent platform to practice and apply your Python skills. By following the steps outlined in this subchapter, you will lay a solid foundation for future projects and gain confidence in your coding abilities, ultimately unlocking the potential of Python in various technological domains.

Interfacing Sensors and Actuators

Interfacing sensors and actuators is a critical aspect of bridging the physical world with digital systems, and Python provides a robust framework for achieving this integration. Sensors are devices that collect data from the environment, such as temperature, light, or motion, while actuators are components that perform actions based on that data, like motors or lights. By employing Python, developers can create applications that not only gather data from various sensors but also respond to that data by controlling actuators, making it an ideal language for projects in the Internet of Things (IoT) and automation.

To begin interfacing sensors and actuators, you will need a microcontroller or single-board computer, such as the Raspberry Pi or Arduino. These devices serve as the bridge between your sensors, actuators, and the Python code you will write. For instance, with a Raspberry Pi, you can connect GPIO (General Purpose Input/Output) pins to sensors and actuators, allowing for easy communication. Python libraries like RPi.GPIO or GPIO Zero simplify the process of reading sensor data and sending signals to actuators, enabling even novice programmers to get started quickly without delving into complex electronics.

When programming sensors, it's vital to understand how to read their output. Different types of sensors have unique communication protocols, such as I2C, SPI, or UART. Python libraries such as Adafruit CircuitPython and PySerial can facilitate these communication methods. For example, with a temperature sensor like the DHT22, you can write a Python script to read the temperature and humidity data at regular intervals. This data can be processed in real-time or stored for further analysis, demonstrating Python's versatility in handling data from sensors effectively.

Once you have successfully gathered data from sensors, the next step is to control actuators based on this information. For instance, if you have a motion sensor that detects movement, you might want to turn on a light as a response. Using Python, you can implement logic that interprets the sensor's output and sends commands to the actuator. Libraries like RPi.GPIO allow you to manipulate the state of GPIO pins easily, enabling you to turn devices on or off with just a few lines of code. This capability is particularly useful in automation projects, where sensors can trigger actuators to create intelligent systems.

In summary, interfacing sensors and actuators using Python opens up a world of possibilities for developers in various technology niches, from IoT to machine learning. By leveraging Python's extensive libraries and straightforward syntax, coders and computer science students can create innovative applications that monitor and interact with the environment. As you gain experience in this area, consider exploring more advanced topics, such as integrating machine learning algorithms to analyze sensor data, which can enhance the functionality and intelligence of your projects.

Data Collection and Analysis in IoT

Data collection and analysis in the Internet of Things (IoT) is a critical component that enables devices to communicate, interact, and optimize their operations. In this context, data is not merely a byproduct of device interaction but a vital asset that drives decision-making processes. IoT devices continuously generate vast amounts of data, including sensor readings, user interactions, and environmental conditions. This data can be collected using various protocols such as MQTT, HTTP, and CoAP, allowing seamless communication between devices and central servers or cloud platforms. Understanding how to effectively gather and manage this data is essential for developers and data analysts looking to leverage the full potential of IoT applications.

Once the data is collected, the next step involves analysis, which transforms raw data into actionable insights. This process typically involves cleaning, filtering, and organizing the data to ensure accuracy and relevance. Python offers several libraries suited for data analysis, such as Pandas, NumPy, and Matplotlib. These tools allow users to manipulate datasets efficiently, perform statistical analyses, and visualize trends and patterns. By harnessing these libraries, coders can create robust data pipelines that facilitate real-time analytics and reporting, ultimately enhancing the functionality of IoT systems.

Moreover, the analysis of IoT data plays a vital role in machine learning applications, enabling predictive analytics and automation. With the help of Python libraries like Scikit-learn and TensorFlow, users can build models that learn from historical data to predict future outcomes. For instance, a smart home system can analyze patterns in energy consumption to optimize power usage, thereby reducing costs and enhancing energy efficiency. This integration of machine learning into IoT not only improves the user experience but also contributes to smarter and more responsive systems.

Data visualization is another essential aspect of data analysis in IoT. Presenting complex data in an easily digestible format allows stakeholders to make informed decisions quickly. Python's visualization libraries, such as Matplotlib, Seaborn, and Plotly, enable developers to create interactive dashboards and visual representations of data. These tools facilitate the identification of trends, anomalies, and correlations within the data, empowering users to derive meaningful insights from their IoT applications. Through effective visualization, organizations can monitor system performance, enhance user engagement, and drive strategic initiatives.

In summary, data collection and analysis are foundational elements of IoT that enable devices to operate intelligently and adaptively. By utilizing Python's extensive ecosystem of libraries, coders and computer science students can effectively gather, analyze, and visualize IoT data, paving the way for innovative solutions across various domains. As the IoT landscape continues to evolve, mastering these skills will be increasingly important for anyone looking to excel in technology-driven fields.

Building IoT Projects

Building IoT projects is an exciting venture that merges the physical world with the digital realm, offering endless possibilities for innovation and automation. At its core, the Internet of Things (IoT) involves connecting everyday objects to the internet, allowing them to send and receive data. Python, with its simplicity and versatility, has become a popular choice for developing IoT applications, making it accessible for coders and computer science students eager to explore this field. Understanding the components of an IoT system, including sensors, actuators, and communication protocols, is essential for anyone looking to embark on IoT projects.

To begin building IoT projects with Python, one must first identify the problem that the project aims to solve. This could range from automating home appliances to monitoring environmental conditions. Once the problem is defined, the next step is to select the appropriate hardware. Popular platforms like Raspberry Pi and Arduino are widely used due to their compatibility with Python and extensive community support. These devices can be easily programmed using Python libraries, making it easier for beginners to bring their ideas to life.

After selecting the hardware, the next phase involves setting up the necessary software environment. Python offers various libraries designed for IoT, such as MicroPython and CircuitPython, which provide the tools needed to interact with hardware components effectively. Additionally, developers can utilize libraries like Flask or Django to create web interfaces for their IoT devices, enabling users to control and monitor their systems remotely. Understanding how to work with APIs and cloud services is also crucial, as many IoT projects rely on these technologies for data storage and processing.

Data collection and analysis are fundamental aspects of IoT projects. Sensors collect data from the environment, which can then be processed using Python's powerful data analysis libraries like Pandas and NumPy. This analysis can lead to valuable insights, allowing users to make informed decisions based on real-time data. For instance, a smart weather station can collect temperature and humidity readings, which can then be visualized using tools like Matplotlib, providing users with intuitive graphs and charts to understand trends.

Lastly, security is a critical consideration in any IoT project. As devices become more interconnected, the risk of cyber threats increases. Implementing security measures, such as data encryption and secure communication protocols, is essential for protecting sensitive information. Python offers various libraries and frameworks to help developers incorporate security practices into their projects. By focusing on building secure and robust IoT applications, coders can ensure that their innovations not only serve their intended purpose but also safeguard users' privacy and data integrity.

Chapter 9: Python for Scientific Computing

Overview of Scientific Computing

Scientific computing is a vital discipline that encompasses the application of computational techniques and algorithms to solve complex scientific and engineering problems. It serves as a bridge between theoretical principles and practical applications, allowing researchers and engineers to simulate phenomena, analyze data, and visualize results using powerful computational tools. Python, with its rich ecosystem of libraries and frameworks, has emerged as a preferred language for scientific computing, enabling users to leverage its capabilities for a wide range of applications.

One of the core components of scientific computing is numerical analysis, which involves the development and implementation of algorithms to obtain numerical solutions to mathematical problems. This includes solving differential equations, performing optimization, and conducting statistical analysis. Python's libraries, such as NumPy and SciPy, provide robust tools for these tasks, allowing users to perform high-level mathematical computations with ease and efficiency. As a result, Python not only simplifies the process of implementing complex algorithms but also enhances the accuracy and reliability of the results produced.

Data visualization plays a crucial role in scientific computing, enabling researchers to interpret and communicate their findings effectively. Python offers powerful visualization libraries like Matplotlib and Seaborn, which facilitate the creation of a wide range of static, animated, and interactive plots. These tools allow users to present their data in a visually appealing manner, making it easier to identify trends, patterns, and outliers. Effective visualization is essential for drawing meaningful conclusions from data and sharing insights with a broader audience, including those who may not have a technical background.

In addition to numerical analysis and visualization, scientific computing often involves the manipulation and analysis of large datasets, a task that has become increasingly important in today's data-driven world. Python's Pandas library is specifically designed for data manipulation and analysis, providing data structures and functions that simplify the process of cleaning, transforming, and aggregating data. With the rise of big data and machine learning, the ability to efficiently handle and analyze vast amounts of information has become a critical skill for coders and computer science students alike.

The integration of scientific computing with other areas of technology, such as machine learning, artificial intelligence, and the Internet of Things (IoT), further expands its relevance and applications. As Python continues to evolve and grow in popularity, its role in scientific computing will only become more significant.

By mastering Python and its scientific computing libraries, aspiring coders and technology enthusiasts can unlock new opportunities, contribute to groundbreaking research, and develop innovative solutions to real-world problems.

Libraries for Scientific Computing: SciPy and NumPy

Libraries for scientific computing in Python are integral tools for anyone looking to delve into data analysis, numerical simulations, or any computational tasks that require precision and efficiency. Two of the most essential libraries in this realm are SciPy and NumPy. While both libraries are closely related, they serve distinct yet complementary purposes. NumPy forms the foundation for numerical computing in Python, providing support for arrays, matrices, and a host of mathematical functions. SciPy builds upon this foundation, offering additional functionality for more complex scientific and engineering problems.

NumPy, short for Numerical Python, is the core library that offers powerful array objects and a variety of operations to manipulate them. At its heart is the ndarray object, which is a fast and flexible container for large data sets in Python. This library enables users to perform element-wise operations on arrays, making it an efficient choice for numerical calculations. It also supports broadcasting, which allows for arithmetic operations on arrays of different shapes, thereby simplifying data manipulation and analysis.

SciPy extends the capabilities of NumPy by providing a wide range of functions that cater to various scientific and engineering fields. Its submodules cover areas such as optimization, integration, interpolation, eigenvalue problems, and more. For instance, if you're working on a project that involves solving differential equations or performing statistical analysis, SciPy offers specialized tools that streamline these tasks. Its integration with NumPy ensures that users can seamlessly transition between basic array manipulations and advanced mathematical operations.

The combination of NumPy and SciPy is particularly beneficial for data analysis and machine learning projects. Many machine learning libraries, such as TensorFlow and scikit-learn, rely on NumPy arrays for data representation and manipulation. This interoperability not only enhances performance but also allows for easier experimentation and testing of algorithms. Furthermore, the extensive documentation and community support for both libraries make them accessible for beginners while providing the depth needed for advanced users.

In summary, mastering NumPy and SciPy is crucial for anyone engaged in scientific computing with Python. Their robust functionalities and efficient data handling capabilities facilitate a wide range of applications, from simple data analysis tasks to complex simulations. As you explore the potential of these libraries, you will find that they are indispensable tools in your coding toolkit, empowering you to tackle real-world problems with confidence and precision. Whether your focus lies in data science, machine learning, or any other computational field, investing time in learning these libraries will significantly enhance your programming proficiency in Python.

Numerical Methods and Simulations

Numerical methods and simulations play an essential role in various fields, particularly in scientific computing, data analysis, and machine learning. These techniques enable coders and computer science students to solve mathematical problems that are often too complex for analytical solutions. Python, with its extensive libraries and frameworks, offers powerful tools for implementing numerical methods and running simulations. Understanding these concepts is crucial for anyone looking to harness Python's full potential in their projects, whether in academia or industry.

One of the foundational numerical methods is the approximation of solutions to equations using iterative techniques. For example, methods such as Newton-Raphson or bisection can be implemented in Python to find roots of nonlinear equations. Python libraries like NumPy and SciPy provide built-in functions that facilitate these processes, allowing programmers to focus on developing their algorithms rather than getting bogged down in the math. By leveraging these tools, students can gain insights into how numerical stability and convergence play critical roles in algorithm design.

Simulations are another vital aspect of numerical methods. They allow users to model real-world systems and analyze their behavior under various conditions. For instance, Monte Carlo simulations can be employed to estimate the probability of different outcomes in uncertain scenarios. This technique is particularly useful in fields such as finance, engineering, and scientific research. Python's libraries, such as Matplotlib for visualization and Pandas for data manipulation, make it easier for coders to generate, analyze, and visualize simulation data, leading to more informed decision-making.

In the context of machine learning, numerical methods are fundamental for training algorithms. Optimization techniques, which are essential for minimizing loss functions in models, heavily rely on numerical analysis. Gradient descent is a popular optimization method that can be efficiently implemented in Python. Understanding how these methods work allows developers to fine-tune their models and improve performance. The interplay between numerical methods and machine learning underscores the importance of a solid grasp of these techniques for aspiring data scientists and machine learning engineers.

Finally, the rise of the Internet of Things (IoT) and automation has further highlighted the need for numerical methods and simulations in Python. As devices become more interconnected, the need for real-time data analysis and decision-making becomes crucial. Implementing simulations to predict system performance or to analyze data from sensors can lead to better control and optimization of IoT systems. Python's versatility allows it to serve as a bridge between data analysis and IoT applications, empowering coders to build systems that are not only functional but also efficient and intelligent.

Data Visualization for Scientific Data

Data visualization is a critical component of scientific data analysis, serving as a bridge between complex numerical information and human understanding. In the realm of Python programming, various libraries facilitate effective visualization, allowing researchers and developers to present their findings in a more digestible and engaging manner. The Python ecosystem offers robust tools such as Matplotlib, Seaborn, and Plotly, which cater to different needs and preferences, making it easier for coders to turn raw data into insightful visual representations.

Matplotlib is one of the most popular libraries for data visualization in Python, renowned for its flexibility and functionality. It allows users to create static, interactive, and animated plots with ease. From line graphs to scatter plots, Matplotlib supports a wide variety of chart types, making it suitable for showcasing trends, distributions, and relationships within scientific data. Coders can customize plots extensively, adjusting elements like colors, labels, and scales to enhance clarity and appeal. This versatility makes Matplotlib an essential tool for anyone involved in data analysis.

Seaborn builds upon Matplotlib's capabilities by providing a higher-level interface for drawing attractive and informative statistical graphics. It simplifies the process of creating complex visualizations, such as heatmaps and categorical plots, which are essential for analyzing multi-dimensional data common in scientific research. Seaborn also integrates seamlessly with Pandas, a powerful data manipulation library, allowing users to visualize data frames directly. This integration streamlines the workflow, enabling coders to focus on the analysis rather than the intricacies of plotting.

For those interested in creating interactive visualizations, Plotly offers a compelling solution. It enables users to build dynamic charts that can be embedded in web applications, making data exploration more engaging. Plotly's support for 3D plots and geographical maps also expands the possibilities for visualizing scientific data. This interactivity is particularly valuable in fields like machine learning and scientific computing, where users can manipulate data visually to gain deeper insights into their models and findings. As the demand for interactive data presentations grows, Plotly stands out as a modern tool for coders looking to elevate their visual storytelling.

Incorporating data visualization into scientific computing not only enhances the understanding of complex data sets but also facilitates communication among stakeholders. It's crucial for coders and computer science students to grasp these visualization techniques, as they are fundamental in transforming abstract data into actionable insights. As technology continues to evolve, mastering these tools will empower developers to contribute meaningfully to fields ranging from artificial intelligence to cybersecurity, ultimately advancing research and innovation across disciplines.

Practical Applications in Scientific Research

Practical applications of Python in scientific research are vast and varied, touching upon numerous fields such as biology, physics, chemistry, and environmental science. Researchers increasingly rely on Python due to its simplicity, readability, and extensive libraries that facilitate complex computations and data analyses. With tools like NumPy and SciPy, scientists can perform mathematical calculations, manipulate large datasets, and conduct simulations with ease. These libraries provide a solid foundation for implementing algorithms and conducting experiments, making Python an invaluable asset in the toolkit of any researcher.

Data analysis is a critical component of scientific research, and Python excels in this area. Libraries such as Pandas enable researchers to handle and analyze structured data effectively. By utilizing Pandas, researchers can clean, transform, and visualize data, allowing them to extract meaningful insights from their experiments. Furthermore, Python's integration with Jupyter Notebooks provides an interactive environment where scientists can document their findings, share their work with others, and visualize results in real time. This combination enhances collaboration and transparency in research, as scientists can present their methodologies and results in an accessible format.

In the realm of machine learning, Python has become the de facto language for developing algorithms that can predict outcomes based on data. Libraries like TensorFlow and scikit-learn allow researchers to create and train models that can analyze patterns in large datasets, making predictions or classifying data points. This capability is especially useful in fields such as genomics, where researchers can identify genetic markers associated with diseases, or in climate science, where predictive models can be developed to assess environmental changes over time. The flexibility of Python makes it easy for researchers to iterate on their models and refine their approaches as new data becomes available.

Python's applicability extends beyond data analysis and machine learning into automation and scripting, which are crucial for handling repetitive tasks in research. Scientists often need to collect data from various sources, process it, and generate reports. Python's scripting capabilities allow researchers to automate these processes, reducing the likelihood of human error and saving valuable time. By writing scripts that interface with databases, APIs, or web scraping tools, researchers can efficiently gather data and focus on interpreting their findings rather than spending hours on manual tasks.

Finally, Python's role in scientific computing cannot be overstated. With libraries like Matplotlib and Seaborn, researchers can create high-quality visualizations that help communicate their results effectively. Visualization is key in scientific research, as it can reveal trends and relationships that might not be immediately apparent from raw data. Additionally, Python's compatibility with various scientific packages and tools allows researchers to integrate their work with other programming languages and systems, fostering a collaborative environment across disciplines. As the demand for reproducibility and transparency in research continues to grow, Python stands out as a powerful language that meets the needs of scientists today.

Chapter 10: Python for Cybersecurity

Introduction to Cybersecurity

In an increasingly digital world, the importance of cybersecurity cannot be overstated. As technology continues to evolve, so do the threats that seek to exploit vulnerabilities in computer systems and networks. Cybersecurity refers to the practices, technologies, and processes designed to protect systems, networks, and data from cyber attacks. Understanding the fundamentals of cybersecurity is essential for anyone involved in technology, including coders, computer science students, and technology enthusiasts. This subchapter will introduce key concepts in cybersecurity, emphasizing its relevance to a variety of applications in the field of Python programming.

One of the primary objectives of cybersecurity is to ensure the confidentiality, integrity, and availability of information. These principles, often referred to as the CIA triad, form the backbone of cybersecurity strategies. Confidentiality ensures that sensitive information is accessed only by authorized individuals, while integrity guarantees that data remains unaltered during storage and transmission. Availability means that information and resources are accessible to authorized users when needed. Understanding these core concepts is vital for developers, as they must consider how their code and applications can be designed to uphold these principles and protect against potential breaches.

As technology advances, so too do the techniques employed by cybercriminals. Common threats include malware, phishing attacks, and denial-of-service attacks. Each of these threats poses unique challenges, requiring a solid understanding of both the attack vectors and the countermeasures available. For instance, Python, a versatile programming language, can be utilized to develop tools for penetration testing, automate security assessments, and analyze malicious code. By gaining knowledge in cybersecurity, coders can better equip themselves to identify vulnerabilities in their own applications and implement robust security measures.

Python's role in cybersecurity extends beyond defensive measures; it also plays a critical part in the development of security solutions. Libraries such as Scapy, Requests, and BeautifulSoup are invaluable for tasks ranging from network scanning to web scraping and data analysis. Moreover, machine learning algorithms can be applied to enhance threat detection and response capabilities. For those interested in cybersecurity, mastering Python not only opens up new avenues for project development but also fosters a deeper understanding of how to create secure applications and systems.

The intersection of Python programming and cybersecurity presents numerous opportunities for innovation and improvement. As more organizations recognize the necessity of cybersecurity in their operations, the demand for skilled professionals in this field continues to rise. By incorporating cybersecurity principles into their coding practices, aspiring developers can contribute to building a safer digital environment. This introductory overview sets the stage for a more in-depth exploration of how Python can be leveraged to address cybersecurity challenges, paving the way for future chapters dedicated to practical applications and techniques.

Using Python for Security Analysis

Using Python for security analysis has gained significant traction among developers and cybersecurity professionals due to its versatility and ease of use. As cyber threats become more sophisticated, the demand for effective security solutions grows. Python, with its rich ecosystem of libraries and frameworks, provides the necessary tools to analyze security vulnerabilities, automate tasks, and develop robust security applications. This subchapter will explore how Python can be utilized in various aspects of security analysis, making it an essential skill for anyone interested in the field.

One of the primary advantages of using Python for security analysis is its extensive library support. Libraries such as Scapy, Requests, and Beautiful Soup allow security analysts to perform network packet manipulation, web scraping, and data extraction with minimal effort. Scapy, for instance, is particularly useful for crafting and sending network packets, making it a valuable tool for penetration testing and network analysis. Additionally, the Requests library simplifies the process of making HTTP requests, enabling users to test web applications for vulnerabilities such as SQL injection and cross-site scripting.

Python's integration capabilities further enhance its effectiveness in security analysis. Many security tools and frameworks are either built with Python or provide Python APIs, allowing analysts to extend their functionalities. For example, tools like Metasploit and OWASP ZAP support Python scripting, enabling users to automate repetitive tasks or customize their workflows. This integration allows for more efficient analysis and the ability to incorporate Python scripts into larger security frameworks, creating a powerful environment for identifying and mitigating threats.

Moreover, Python's readability and simplicity make it an ideal language for prototyping and developing security tools. When faced with urgent security issues, analysts can quickly write scripts to address vulnerabilities or automate responses to incidents. The ability to iterate rapidly on ideas and implement solutions in real-time is crucial in the fast-paced world of cybersecurity. Python's syntax, which closely resembles natural language, allows beginners to grasp concepts quickly, making it accessible to those who may be new to programming.

Lastly, the growing community of Python enthusiasts in the cybersecurity domain fosters collaboration and knowledge sharing. Numerous open-source projects and resources are available, enabling coders and students to learn from existing tools and contribute to ongoing developments. Engaging with this community not only enhances individual skills but also helps in staying updated with the latest trends and techniques in security analysis. As cybersecurity continues to evolve, leveraging Python will undoubtedly remain a critical asset for those aspiring to make a mark in this dynamic field.

Writing Scripts for Network Scanning

Writing scripts for network scanning is an essential skill for those interested in cybersecurity, network administration, and systems management. Network scanning allows you to discover active devices on a network, identify open ports, and determine potential vulnerabilities. By using Python, you can automate these tasks to enhance efficiency and improve your understanding of network security. In this subchapter, we will explore how to create a simple network scanner using Python, focusing on libraries and techniques that will help you gather valuable information about your network.

To begin with, you'll need to familiarize yourself with some key Python libraries crucial for network scanning. The `socket` library is fundamental, as it provides a way to connect to other machines over a network. Additionally, the `scapy` library is a powerful tool for packet manipulation and network scanning. It allows you to send, sniff, and dissect network packets, making it an excellent choice for more advanced scanning tasks.

Installing these libraries is straightforward using pip, Python's package manager, and you can easily integrate them into your scripts to perform various network scanning operations.

Creating a basic network scanner involves writing a script that can ping a range of IP addresses to determine which devices are active. By leveraging the `socket` library, you can attempt to establish a connection to each IP address within a specified subnet. If a connection is successful, it indicates that a device is online. You can also implement multi-threading to speed up the scanning process, allowing your script to check multiple addresses simultaneously. This optimization is crucial for efficiency, especially in larger networks where scanning can take considerable time if done sequentially.

In addition to simply identifying active devices, a more comprehensive network scanner can also check for open ports on each active device. This information is vital for assessing the security posture of your network. By utilizing the `socket` library to attempt connections to various ports, you can identify which services are running on each device. This step not only helps in understanding the network's architecture but also highlights potential vulnerabilities that could be exploited by malicious actors. Be mindful, however, that scanning networks without permission may violate legal and ethical guidelines.

Finally, once you've developed your network scanning script, it's essential to test and refine it. Start by scanning a small subnet where you have authorization, enabling you to observe the results and make adjustments as needed. Consider implementing logging features to record the scan results for further analysis. Furthermore, you can enhance your script by adding functionalities such as scheduling scans, generating reports, or even integrating it with alerting mechanisms. By developing your network scanning skills through Python, you equip yourself with valuable tools for both cybersecurity and network management, positioning yourself favorably in the tech industry.

Automated Vulnerability Testing

Automated vulnerability testing is a critical component in the realm of cybersecurity, leveraging Python's extensive libraries and frameworks to identify potential security flaws in applications and systems. In the context of Python programming, automated vulnerability testing involves the use of scripts and tools that can scan codebases for common vulnerabilities, misconfigurations, and other security issues without the need for manual intervention. This not only enhances efficiency but also allows developers and security professionals to focus their efforts on resolving identified vulnerabilities rather than spending excessive time on the testing process itself.

One popular library for automated vulnerability testing in Python is Bandit, which specializes in identifying common security issues in Python code. Bandit scans the code to detect potential vulnerabilities such as hardcoded passwords, weak cryptography, and insecure function calls. By integrating Bandit into the development workflow, coders can ensure that security considerations are addressed early in the software development lifecycle, promoting a proactive approach to security rather than a reactive one. This integration can be seamlessly achieved using continuous integration/continuous deployment (CI/CD) pipelines, enhancing the overall security posture of applications.

Another valuable tool within the Python ecosystem is OWASP ZAP (Zed Attack Proxy), which provides automated scanning capabilities for web applications. By utilizing ZAP's API, developers can script automated scans that look for vulnerabilities such as SQL injection, cross-site scripting (XSS), and other web-specific security issues. This tool not only allows for the identification of vulnerabilities in existing applications but also serves as a learning opportunity for students and new coders to understand how various attack vectors function. By experimenting with these tools, individuals can gain practical insights into secure coding practices.

For those focused on data analysis or machine learning, automated vulnerability testing can also extend to the datasets used in these applications. Python libraries like pandas can be employed to analyze data for anomalies or patterns that may indicate security issues, such as data breaches or leaks. By automating these analyses, data scientists can ensure the integrity of their datasets while also maintaining an awareness of potential security implications. This cross-disciplinary approach underscores the importance of security in all aspects of software development and data handling.

In summary, automated vulnerability testing plays a vital role in enhancing the security of software applications. By leveraging Python's robust libraries and tools, coders and computer science students can develop a strong understanding of security principles while implementing effective testing strategies. As technology continues to evolve and cyber threats become increasingly sophisticated, the ability to automate vulnerability testing will remain an essential skill for anyone involved in technology, from web development to artificial intelligence and beyond.

Real-world Cybersecurity Scenarios

Real-world cybersecurity scenarios can provide invaluable insights into the complexities and challenges faced by professionals in the field. These scenarios often highlight the importance of coding skills, specifically in Python, as a tool for developing effective cybersecurity solutions. By understanding these situations, coders and computer science students can better appreciate how their programming knowledge can be applied to protect systems, networks, and sensitive information from malicious attacks.

One prevalent scenario involves the detection and response to phishing attacks. Phishing is a technique used by cybercriminals to deceive individuals into revealing personal information, such as passwords or credit card numbers. Python can be utilized to build scripts that analyze email headers and content, filtering out potential phishing attempts. For instance, by employing libraries like Beautiful Soup for web scraping or regular expressions for pattern matching, a coder can automate the process of identifying suspicious emails, providing a proactive defense mechanism against these common threats.

Another critical scenario revolves around the analysis of security logs to identify potential breaches. Large organizations generate vast amounts of log data, which can be overwhelming to analyze manually. Python's data analysis libraries, such as Pandas and NumPy, enable the parsing and visualization of this data effectively. Coders can write scripts to search for anomalies, such as unusually high login attempts or access to sensitive files outside of normal business hours. By automating this analysis, organizations can respond swiftly to potential security incidents and mitigate risks before they escalate.

In the domain of web development, securing applications against common vulnerabilities is paramount. For example, cross-site scripting (XSS) and SQL injection attacks can compromise the integrity of web applications. Python frameworks like Flask or Django come equipped with built-in security features, but additional coding efforts are often necessary to fortify these applications further. Developers can write custom validation scripts to sanitize user input, ensuring data integrity and preventing malicious code from being executed. This practice not only enhances the security of the application but also fosters a culture of security awareness among developers.

Finally, the rise of Internet of Things (IoT) devices presents unique cybersecurity challenges. With countless devices connected to the internet, each poses potential vulnerabilities. Python can be instrumental in developing monitoring tools that track the behavior of IoT devices, identifying unusual patterns that may indicate a compromise. For instance, a coder can create scripts to analyze data traffic from smart home devices, looking for signs of unauthorized access or anomalies in expected behavior. This proactive approach can help secure IoT ecosystems, ensuring that users' data and privacy remain intact.

By exploring these real-world cybersecurity scenarios, coders and students can recognize the crucial role that Python plays in implementing effective cybersecurity measures. Understanding these scenarios not only enriches their coding skills but also equips them with the knowledge necessary to tackle the myriad challenges posed by an ever-evolving digital landscape.

Chapter 11: Hotkeys and Commands in Python Development Environments

Hotkeys and Commands in Python Development Environments

When working with **Python**, mastering **hotkeys and commands** in popular development environments can significantly improve efficiency. Below is a list of commonly used hotkeys for some of the most popular **Python IDEs and text editors**, including **PyCharm, VS Code, Jupyter Notebook, and Terminal/Command Line**.

---

1. PyCharm Hotkeys (JetBrains IDEs)

PyCharm is one of the most widely used **Python IDEs**, offering powerful features like debugging, refactoring, and intelligent code assistance.

Basic Navigation & Editing

Ctrl + N → Open Class

Ctrl + Shift + N → Open File

Ctrl + Shift + A → Search for Actions/Settings

Ctrl + B (Cmd + B on Mac) → Go to Definition

Ctrl + E → Recent Files

Alt + ← / Alt + → → Navigate Back/Forward

Code Assistance & Refactoring

Ctrl + Space → Auto-complete

Ctrl + Shift + Enter → Smart Auto-completion

Ctrl + Alt + L → Reformat Code

Ctrl + Alt + O → Optimize Imports

Shift + F6 → Rename Symbol

Running & Debugging

Shift + F10 → Run Script

Shift + F9 → Debug Script

Ctrl + F8 → Toggle Breakpoint

Alt + Shift + F9 → Debug Configurations

---

2. VS Code (Visual Studio Code) Hotkeys

VS Code is a lightweight yet powerful **Python editor**, especially when used with extensions like **Python, Jupyter, and Pylance**.

Basic Editing

Ctrl + P → Quick Open (Search Files)

Ctrl + Shift + P → Command Palette

Ctrl + / → Toggle Comment

Alt + ↑ / Alt + ↓ → Move Line Up/Down

Ctrl + Shift + K → Delete Line

Code Assistance & Navigation

F12 → Go to Definition

Ctrl + Shift + O → Go to Symbol

Ctrl + Shift + F → Global Search

Ctrl + Shift + M → Show Problems (Errors, Warnings)

Running & Debugging

F5 → Start Debugging

Shift + F5 → Stop Debugging

Ctrl + ` (Backtick) → Open Integrated Terminal

Ctrl + Shift + ` (Backtick) → Open New Terminal

---

3. Jupyter Notebook Hotkeys

Jupyter Notebooks are widely used for **data science, machine learning, and interactive Python programming**.

Notebook Modes

Esc → Switch to Command Mode

Enter → Switch to Edit Mode

Cell Management

A → Insert Cell Above

B → Insert Cell Below

DD (Double D) → Delete Cell

Shift + M → Merge Cells

Code Execution

Shift + Enter → Run Cell and Move to Next

Ctrl + Enter → Run Cell Without Moving

Alt + Enter → Run Cell and Insert Below

---

4. Python Terminal / Command Line Shortcuts

For those who use **Python in the terminal (interactive mode, scripts, or virtual environments)**, these commands are essential.

Running Python Scripts

python script.py → Run Python Script

python -m module_name → Run a Python Module

python -c "print('Hello, World!')" → Execute Inline Python

Virtual Environment Management

python -m venv env_name → Create Virtual Environment

source env_name/bin/activate (Mac/Linux) → Activate Virtual Environment

env_name\Scripts\activate (Windows) → Activate Virtual Environment

deactivate → Deactivate Virtual Environment

Package Management with pip

pip install package_name → Install Package

pip uninstall package_name → Remove Package

pip list → Show Installed Packages

pip freeze > requirements.txt → Save Installed Packages

pip install -r requirements.txt → Install Packages from File

Mastering **hotkeys and commands** in your preferred **Python development environment** can dramatically enhance **efficiency, debugging, and workflow management**. Whether you're using **PyCharm, VS Code, Jupyter, or the Terminal**, these shortcuts will help you **code faster and smarter**. 🚀

Chapter 12: Introduction to Python Syntax

Overview of Python

Python is a high-level, interpreted programming language known for its simplicity and readability. Created by Guido van Rossum and first released in 1991, Python has grown to become one of the most popular programming languages globally. Its design philosophy emphasizes code readability and the use of significant whitespace, making it an ideal choice for beginners and experienced developers alike. Python's versatility allows it to be used for various applications, including web development, data analysis, artificial intelligence, scientific computing, and more. This flexibility, combined with an extensive standard library and a vibrant ecosystem of third-party packages, makes Python a go-to language for many developers.

One of the key features of Python is its dynamic typing system, which allows developers to define variables without explicitly declaring their data types. This characteristic simplifies the coding process, enabling faster development cycles. Python supports multiple data types, including integers, floats, strings, lists, tuples, dictionaries, and sets, providing a rich set of tools for data manipulation. Understanding these data types is essential for any programmer, as they form the foundation upon which more complex structures and algorithms are built. The language's syntax is designed to be intuitive and straightforward, which helps reduce the learning curve for new coders.

Control flow and looping mechanisms in Python are vital components that allow developers to execute code conditionally and repeatedly. The language provides several constructs, including if statements, for loops, and while loops, enabling programmers to create dynamic and responsive applications. These control structures are essential for building logic into programs, allowing them to respond to various inputs and conditions efficiently. Mastering these flow control techniques is crucial for writing effective and efficient Python code, as they directly impact program functionality and performance.

Python also boasts a rich set of built-in functions and libraries that enhance its capabilities. These libraries, such as NumPy for numerical computations, pandas for data manipulation, and Flask for web development, provide pre-built solutions that save time and effort. Familiarity with these built-in functions and libraries allows coders to leverage Python's full potential, enabling them to focus on solving problems rather than reinventing the wheel. Additionally, Python's extensive documentation and community support make it easier for developers to find resources and examples to aid in their coding endeavors.

As coding practices evolve, adhering to best practices for writing clean Python code becomes increasingly important. This includes following conventions for naming variables, structuring projects, and documenting code effectively. Utilizing integrated development environments (IDEs) and mastering hotkeys can significantly enhance coding efficiency, allowing programmers to navigate and manipulate codebases swiftly. As developers familiarize themselves with common Python shortcuts for data manipulation and other tasks, they will find that the language not only promotes productivity but also fosters a collaborative environment where code can be easily understood and maintained by others.

Importance of Syntax in Programming

Syntax in programming serves as the backbone of code structure, dictating how statements are formed and organized to create functional programs. In Python, the importance of syntax is particularly pronounced due to its emphasis on readability and simplicity. A well-structured syntax not only facilitates easier debugging but also enhances collaboration among developers. Understanding Python's syntax allows coders to write cleaner, more efficient code, making it easier to spot errors and optimize performance.

The syntax rules of Python govern how various elements such as variables, data types, and control flow statements interact with one another. For instance, the correct use of indentation is critical in Python, as it defines the scope of loops and functions. This unique approach to syntax helps prevent common errors that may arise from misaligned braces or semicolons, which are prevalent in other programming languages. As a result, Python syntax promotes a more intuitive coding experience, allowing programmers to focus on problem-solving rather than getting bogged down in complex syntactical structures.

Moreover, a strong grasp of syntax aids in the effective use of Python's built-in functions and libraries. Many of these functions are designed to work seamlessly with Python's syntax, enabling developers to leverage powerful tools to manipulate data and perform computations efficiently. By adhering to proper syntax, programmers can easily integrate these functions into their code, ultimately streamlining development processes and enhancing productivity. This ability to utilize Python's extensive libraries effectively is crucial for coders aiming to maximize their coding efficiency and effectiveness.

Control flow and looping mechanisms are another area where syntax plays a vital role. The proper structuring of conditional statements and loops determines the flow of execution in a Python program. Understanding the syntax associated with these constructs allows developers to implement complex logic with clarity and precision. As coders become more familiar with Python's syntax, they can manipulate control flow statements to create more dynamic applications, ultimately leading to more versatile and responsive software solutions.

Lastly, embracing best practices for writing clean Python code heavily relies on an understanding of syntax. Clean code not only adheres to syntactic norms but also promotes maintainability and readability. By following established conventions and using consistent syntax, programmers can ensure that their code is accessible to others, facilitating easier collaboration and future modifications. In an environment where teamwork is crucial, a solid foundation in syntax becomes indispensable for creating high-quality, professional-grade software.

Getting Started with Python

Getting started with Python is an exciting journey into one of the most versatile and widely-used programming languages today. Python's simplicity and readability make it an ideal choice for both beginners and experienced coders. To effectively dive into Python, it is essential to understand its core syntax and structure, which serve as the foundation for writing efficient and clean code. This chapter will guide you through the essentials of Python syntax, providing a solid grounding before exploring more advanced topics.

When beginning with Python, the first step is to familiarize yourself with the various data types. Python supports several built-in data types, including integers, floats, strings, and booleans. Understanding these data types is crucial, as they determine how data is stored and manipulated within a program. For instance, integers and floats are used for numerical calculations, while strings are essential for text processing. Python also offers data structures such as lists, tuples, sets, and dictionaries, which allow for organized data management and manipulation.

Variables in Python play a significant role in storing and referencing data. Unlike some programming languages, Python does not require explicit declaration of variable types; it automatically infers the type based on the assigned value. This dynamic typing feature simplifies the coding process, making it easier to write and maintain code. However, it is vital to follow best practices for naming variables to ensure code readability and prevent confusion. Meaningful variable names enhance the clarity of your code, allowing others and your future self to understand its purpose more easily.

Control flow and looping mechanisms are fundamental components of Python programming. These constructs enable developers to dictate the order in which code executes, manage repetitive tasks, and handle decisions within a program. The primary control flow statements in Python include if, elif, and else, while loops and for loops are powerful tools for iterating over sequences or executing a block of code multiple times. Mastering these constructs is essential for developing robust applications and automating repetitive processes efficiently.

Finally, leveraging Python's built-in functions and libraries can significantly enhance productivity and streamline coding efforts. Python comes equipped with a rich standard library that provides numerous modules and functions for tasks ranging from file I/O to mathematical calculations. Familiarizing yourself with commonly used libraries, such as NumPy for numerical computations and Pandas for data manipulation, will empower you to tackle complex tasks with ease. Additionally, exploring various Integrated Development Environments (IDEs) and their associated hotkeys can further improve coding efficiency, allowing you to focus on writing clean and effective Python code.

Chapter 13: Python Core Basics and Hot Keys

Understanding Python Syntax Basics

Understanding Python syntax basics is essential for anyone looking to master the language and its applications. Python syntax serves as the foundation for writing clean and efficient code, and it defines how various commands and functions are structured. Unlike many programming languages, Python emphasizes readability and simplicity, making it an ideal choice for both beginners and seasoned programmers. Familiarizing oneself with Python syntax allows developers to write code that not only executes correctly but is also easy to maintain and understand.

At its core, Python syntax includes keywords, operators, and punctuation that govern how code is interpreted. Keywords such as 'def,' 'if,' 'else,' and 'for' are integral to defining functions, making decisions, and creating loops. Understanding how to use these keywords correctly is vital for creating effective control flow structures. Additionally, operators like addition (+), subtraction (-), and comparison (==) play a critical role in manipulating data types and facilitating logical operations. Mastering these elements ensures that programmers can craft functional and efficient code.

Whitespace and indentation are particularly unique aspects of Python syntax. Unlike many other programming languages that use braces or keywords to denote code blocks, Python relies on indentation to signal the start and end of a block of code. This design choice enhances code readability, but it also requires developers to be meticulous in their formatting. A consistent approach to indentation not only helps avoid syntax errors but also contributes to cleaner code, which is easier to navigate and debug.

Data types are another crucial element of Python syntax. Python supports various data types, including integers, floats, strings, and booleans. Each data type has its specific syntax for declaration and manipulation. For example, strings can be created using single or double quotes, while lists are defined using square brackets. Understanding the appropriate syntax for each data type is essential for effective data manipulation and control flow. Additionally, Python's dynamic typing allows variables to change types during execution, which is an important concept to grasp for writing flexible and robust code.

Finally, leveraging Python's built-in functions and libraries can significantly enhance coding efficiency while adhering to proper syntax. Functions like 'print,' 'len,' and 'range' come pre-installed with Python and can be utilized without the need for extensive setup. Furthermore, the vast array of libraries available, such as NumPy and pandas, provides additional functionality that can streamline data manipulation tasks. By mastering Python syntax basics, programmers can not only improve their coding proficiency but also harness the power of Python's extensive ecosystem to tackle complex programming challenges effectively.

Common Hot Keys for Python Programming

In Python programming, efficiency is key, and understanding common hot keys can significantly enhance productivity. The use of hot keys, or keyboard shortcuts, allows programmers to streamline their workflow, reduce reliance on the mouse, and navigate their coding environment more effectively. This practice is especially beneficial in Integrated Development Environments (IDEs) and code editors, where the ability to quickly access features can make a substantial difference in coding speed and accuracy.

First and foremost, familiarizing oneself with navigation shortcuts is essential. For instance, in popular IDEs like PyCharm or VS Code, using Ctrl + N can quickly open a new file, while Ctrl + O allows for opening existing files. Additionally, the ability to switch between tabs using Ctrl + Tab can help maintain focus on multiple files without losing context. These navigation hot keys are foundational for any coder looking to improve their efficiency, enabling them to move fluidly between different parts of a project.

Editing shortcuts are equally important in Python programming. Hot keys such as Ctrl + C for copy, Ctrl + V for paste, and Ctrl + Z for undo are universal across many platforms, making them easy to remember. However, IDEs often have additional shortcuts that can enhance the editing experience even further. For example, using Ctrl + D to duplicate a line or selection can save time when writing repetitive code. Similarly, Ctrl + / can comment or uncomment the selected lines, providing a quick way to manage code during development and debugging.

Moreover, utilizing shortcuts for code formatting and refactoring is crucial for maintaining clean and readable code. For instance, in many Python IDEs, pressing Ctrl + Alt + L can automatically format the code according to PEP 8 standards, ensuring that it adheres to Python's style guidelines. Refactoring shortcuts, such as Shift + F6 for renaming a variable or function, allow for quick adjustments without the risk of manually missing instances of the name throughout the codebase. These features not only save time but also promote best practices in writing clean code.

Lastly, understanding the importance of hot keys for executing and debugging code can dramatically improve a coder's efficiency. The F5 key is commonly used to run the current script, while F9 can set breakpoints in the code for debugging purposes. These shortcuts are indispensable for testing code snippets and troubleshooting issues, allowing programmers to quickly identify and fix errors. Mastering these hot keys ultimately leads to a more efficient coding experience and enhances the overall quality of the programming work produced.

Setting Up Your Python Environment

Setting up your Python environment is a crucial first step for any coder looking to effectively harness the power of Python. To begin, the choice of an Integrated Development Environment (IDE) can significantly impact your coding experience. Popular options such as PyCharm, Visual Studio Code, and Jupyter Notebook cater to different needs. PyCharm offers a rich feature set suitable for large projects, while Visual Studio Code is known for its lightweight nature and extensive plugin ecosystem. Jupyter Notebook, on the other hand, excels in data science and educational contexts, providing an interactive interface for running code snippets alongside rich text documentation.

Once you have selected your IDE, the next step is to install Python itself. You can download the latest version of Python from the official Python website. The installation process is straightforward on most operating systems, with options to add Python to your system PATH, which is essential for running Python scripts from the command line. It's advisable to install the latest stable version to ensure access to the most recent features and security updates. After installation, you can verify the setup by opening a terminal or command prompt and typing "python --version" to confirm the successful installation.

In addition to Python, setting up a virtual environment is highly recommended, especially when working on multiple projects with varying dependencies. A virtual environment allows you to create isolated spaces for each project, ensuring that library versions do not clash. You can create a virtual environment using the built-in `venv` module by navigating to your project directory and executing the command "python -m venv myenv." Activating this environment will allow you to install packages such as NumPy, Pandas, or Flask without affecting other projects.

Package management is another vital aspect of setting up your Python environment. The Python Package Index (PyPI) hosts a wealth of libraries that enhance Python's functionality. You can manage these packages using pip, Python's package manager. After activating your virtual environment, you can install packages with the command "pip install package_name." Keeping your dependencies up to date is crucial for maintaining a stable development environment, so regularly check for updates using "pip list --outdated" and upgrade packages as necessary.

Finally, configuring your IDE with shortcuts and best practices can drastically improve your coding efficiency. Most IDEs offer customizable hotkeys for common actions such as running code, debugging, and navigating through files. Familiarizing yourself with these shortcuts can save time, allowing you to focus more on writing clean and effective code. Additionally, adopting best practices such as consistent naming conventions, code comments, and utilizing version control systems like Git will enhance collaboration and maintainability in your projects..

Chapter 14: Python Syntax and Structure

Basic Syntax Rules

In the realm of Python programming, understanding basic syntax rules is crucial for writing effective and efficient code. Syntax in Python refers to the set of rules that defines the combinations of symbols and keywords that are considered to be correctly structured programs. Unlike some other programming languages, Python emphasizes readability and simplicity, making it an excellent choice for both beginners and experienced developers. Familiarity with these syntax rules not only aids in avoiding errors but also enhances the overall coding experience by making the code more maintainable.

One fundamental aspect of Python's syntax is its reliance on indentation to define the structure of the code. Unlike languages that use braces or keywords to denote code blocks, Python uses indentation levels to determine the grouping of statements. This means that consistent indentation is necessary for the proper execution of the code. For example, when defining functions, loops, or conditionals, all statements within those blocks must be indented the same amount. This approach encourages developers to write cleaner and more organized code, reducing the likelihood of syntax-related bugs.

Another critical syntax rule involves the use of colons and parentheses. In Python, colons are used to indicate the start of an indented block following control flow statements such as 'if', 'for', and 'while'. Similarly, parentheses are crucial when calling functions, defining tuples, or grouping expressions. For instance, a function definition begins with the 'def' keyword followed by the function name and parentheses that can contain parameters. Mastering the correct placement and use of these syntactical elements is essential for writing well-structured Python code.

Moreover, Python's syntax is designed to support a variety of data types seamlessly. Variables in Python do not require explicit declaration to define their type; instead, they are dynamically typed. This means that the type of a variable is inferred from the value it is assigned. For instance, assigning an integer value to a variable allows it to be treated as an integer without any explicit type declaration. Understanding how to work with different data types, such as strings, lists, tuples, and dictionaries, while adhering to the syntax rules is fundamental for any coder looking to manipulate data effectively.

Finally, built-in functions and libraries in Python often come with their own set of syntactical requirements. For instance, using libraries like 'math' or 'datetime' requires understanding how to import these modules correctly and utilize their functions within the established syntax rules. Familiarity with these rules not only improves code efficiency but also enables programmers to leverage Python's powerful standard library for various applications. By adhering to these basic syntax guidelines, programmers can enhance their coding practices, leading to cleaner, more efficient, and bug-free code.

Indentation and Code Blocks

Indentation in Python is a fundamental aspect of the language's syntax that distinguishes it from many other programming languages. Unlike languages that use braces or keywords to define code blocks, Python relies on indentation to create structure and hierarchy within the code. This means that the level of indentation determines how statements are grouped together and how they relate to one another within control structures like loops and conditionals. For example, in a function definition or a loop, the lines of code that are indented under the header form a block that is executed together, which is essential for maintaining the intended logic of the program.

The significance of proper indentation cannot be overstated. A common pitfall for new programmers is inconsistent indentation, which can lead to unexpected behavior or errors during execution. Python enforces indentation strictly, and any deviation from the expected structure results in an IndentationError. To avoid such issues, it is crucial to choose a consistent indentation style, whether using spaces or tabs, and to stick with it throughout your code. The Python community generally recommends using four spaces per indentation level, which enhances readability and maintains consistency across different codebases.

Code blocks in Python are created by indenting lines of code that follow certain statements, such as function definitions, loops, and conditional statements. For instance, when defining a function, the body of the function must be indented relative to the function's declaration. Similarly, in an if statement, any code that should execute when the condition is true must also be indented. This structure allows developers to quickly understand the flow of control in a program, as the indentation visually represents the logical grouping of code.

In addition to enhancing readability, proper indentation also facilitates collaboration among developers. When multiple programmers work on the same codebase, adherence to indentation standards helps ensure that everyone can read and understand each other's code without confusion. This is particularly important in larger projects where numerous contributors may be involved. By maintaining consistent indentation practices, teams can avoid merge conflicts and improve the overall maintainability of the code.

To further streamline the coding process, many Integrated Development Environments (IDEs) and text editors offer features that help manage indentation automatically. These tools can convert tabs to spaces, ensure that the correct number of spaces is used for indentation, and even visually highlight blocks of code.

Familiarizing oneself with these features can significantly enhance coding efficiency and help programmers focus on logic and functionality rather than formatting. Emphasizing best practices for indentation and code block structuring is essential for writing clean, efficient, and error-free Python code.

Comments and Documentation

Comments and documentation are essential components of writing clean, maintainable code in Python. They serve as a guide for both the original developer and anyone else who may encounter the code in the future. Comments are non-executable lines in the code that provide context or explanations about what a particular section of code does. In Python, comments can be created using the hash symbol (#), which indicates that everything following it on that line will not be executed. Properly placed comments can clarify complex logic, making it easier for others to understand your thought process and the purpose behind your code.

Documentation, on the other hand, refers to the more formalized descriptions of modules, classes, methods, and functions within the code. Python encourages the use of docstrings, which are special string literals that describe what a function or class does. These docstrings are defined using triple quotes and can span multiple lines, making them ideal for providing detailed explanations. They can include information about parameters, return values, exceptions raised, and examples of usage. This practice not only benefits others who read your code but also allows tools like Sphinx to generate documentation automatically for your projects.

When writing comments, it is important to strike a balance between being informative and concise. Overly verbose comments can clutter the code and detract from its readability, while too few comments may leave the reader confused about the code's intent. Aim to explain why something is done, rather than what is done, as the code itself should ideally convey the latter. For example, instead of commenting on a straightforward loop that iterates over a list, focus on the purpose of that loop within the context of the program. This approach makes your code cleaner and easier to follow.

In addition to inline comments and docstrings, Python developers should also consider using external documentation tools and practices. Version control systems like Git can be used to maintain a changelog that tracks modifications to the codebase. Moreover, README files can provide an overview of the project, installation instructions, usage guidelines, and contribution details. These documents can enhance the onboarding process for new team members and serve as a reference for users who want to understand how to interact with the code.

Finally, adhering to best practices for comments and documentation can greatly improve the quality of Python code. Following conventions such as PEP 8 for style and PEP 257 for docstring conventions ensures consistency and professionalism in your coding projects. Regularly updating comments and documentation as the code evolves is equally important, as outdated information can lead to confusion and errors. By prioritizing comments and documentation, Python programmers can create a more collaborative environment, foster better communication, and ultimately produce code that stands the test of time.

Chapter 15: Data Types and Variables in Python

Introduction to Data Types

In Python, data types are fundamental concepts that define the nature of the data being processed. Understanding data types is crucial for coders and computer programmers, as they determine how data is stored, manipulated, and interacted with within the programming environment. Python offers several built-in data types, each serving distinct purposes and enabling various operations to be performed efficiently. The main categories of data types include numeric types, sequences, mappings, sets, and boolean types, each with unique characteristics and use cases.

Numeric types in Python consist of integers, floating-point numbers, and complex numbers, allowing for precise mathematical calculations. Integers are whole numbers without a fractional component, while floating-point numbers accommodate decimal points and represent real numbers. Complex numbers extend this functionality by including both a real and an imaginary part. Coders should be familiar with these numeric types to perform arithmetic operations, comparisons, and numerical analyses effectively, as they form the building blocks for more complex programming tasks.

Sequences are another essential category of data types in Python, encompassing lists, tuples, and strings. Lists are mutable, allowing for dynamic changes, such as adding or removing elements, while tuples are immutable and provide a fixed collection of items. Strings, on the other hand, are used to represent text and are also immutable. Understanding how to manipulate these sequences is vital for managing collections of data, iterating through items, and applying various built-in functions that enhance programming efficiency and readability.

Mappings, specifically dictionaries in Python, provide a powerful way to store and retrieve data in key-value pairs. This data structure allows programmers to access values based on unique keys, making it an efficient choice for scenarios where fast lookup times are essential. Coders should leverage dictionaries for tasks such as configuration settings, data representation, and when dealing with associative arrays, as they facilitate quick data access and modifications.

Finally, boolean types represent truth values, either True or False, and play a critical role in control flow and decision-making within Python programs. Understanding how to utilize boolean types effectively can enhance coding strategies, allowing for the implementation of conditional statements and loops that govern the program's execution path. A solid grasp of data types equips programmers to write clearer, more efficient code, leveraging Python's capabilities to manage and manipulate data seamlessly.

Working with Variables

In Python, variables serve as essential building blocks for storing and manipulating data. A variable in Python is essentially a name that references a value stored in memory. Unlike many other programming languages, Python does not require explicit declaration of variable types. Instead, the type of the variable is inferred from the value assigned to it. This dynamic typing feature allows for greater flexibility but also necessitates a clear understanding of how to manage and utilize variables effectively. For example, you can easily assign an integer to a variable, and later reassign it to a string without any errors, which showcases Python's versatility.

When working with variables, it's crucial to follow naming conventions to maintain clarity and readability in your code. Variable names should be descriptive and adhere to the rules set by Python’s syntax. This includes starting with a letter or underscore, followed by letters, numbers, or underscores, and avoiding the use of reserved keywords. Adopting conventions such as using lowercase letters for variable names, and underscores to separate words (known as snake_case), can enhance the readability of your code, making it easier for others (and yourself) to understand the purpose of each variable at a glance.

Understanding the scope of variables is equally important. In Python, variables can have local or global scope. A local variable is one that is defined within a function and is only accessible within that function, while a global variable is defined outside any function and can be accessed from anywhere in the code. This distinction can affect the behavior of your program, particularly in more complex applications where functions may interact with shared data. Utilizing global variables can simplify certain tasks but should be done with caution to avoid unintended side effects.

Python also provides a range of built-in functions that work seamlessly with variables, allowing for easy manipulation and transformation of data. Functions such as `len()`, `type()`, and `str()` enable you to gauge the properties of your variables and convert between different data types. Additionally, understanding how to use Python's list and dictionary comprehensions can lead to more efficient and concise code. These features not only enhance performance but also align with best practices for writing clean and maintainable Python code.

As you become more comfortable with variables in Python, consider exploring advanced techniques such as variable unpacking and the use of data structures like lists, tuples, and dictionaries. Mastering these concepts will empower you to write more sophisticated programs that can handle complex data efficiently. Furthermore, familiarizing yourself with IDE features and shortcuts can significantly streamline your coding process, allowing you to focus on problem-solving rather than syntax errors. Emphasizing clarity, consistency, and efficiency in your variable management will contribute to better coding practices and improved program performance in your Python projects.

Type Conversion and Casting

Type conversion and casting are essential concepts in Python that enable programmers to manipulate variables and ensure data compatibility across different operations. Python is a dynamically typed language, meaning variable types are determined at runtime. This flexibility allows developers to write code without explicitly declaring data types, but it also necessitates a solid understanding of how to convert between types when required. The built-in functions provided by Python facilitate this process, enabling seamless integration of various data types.

Explicit type conversion, often referred to as casting, occurs when a programmer converts one data type to another. This is done using functions such as int(), float(), str(), and others. For instance, converting a floating-point number to an integer can be accomplished with the int() function. This function truncates the decimal portion, effectively rounding down the value. Similarly, converting an integer to a string can be achieved using str(), which is particularly useful when concatenating numbers with other strings for user output.

Implicit type conversion, on the other hand, is handled automatically by Python where possible. For example, when performing arithmetic operations involving both integers and floats, Python will implicitly convert the integer to a float to ensure that the operation maintains precision. This automatic type promotion helps prevent errors related to incompatible data types but can also lead to unintended consequences if not properly managed. Understanding the nuances of implicit conversion is vital for writing robust code that behaves as expected.

Type conversion is particularly important when working with user input. Since input from the user is always received as a string, developers must explicitly convert this input to the desired data type before performing operations. For example, when a program requires a numeric input, the string must be converted to an integer or float using the appropriate casting function. Failure to do so can result in runtime errors or incorrect program behavior, highlighting the importance of validating and converting user input correctly.

In summary, mastering type conversion and casting is crucial for Python programmers. It ensures data integrity and compatibility across various operations, facilitating the development of efficient and error-free code. By utilizing built-in functions for explicit casting and understanding the implications of implicit conversion, developers can navigate the complexities of data types, leading to cleaner and more maintainable code. As you enhance your skills in Python, pay close attention to these type conversion techniques to improve your coding efficiency and effectiveness.

Chapter 16: Control Flow and Looping Mechanisms

Conditional Statements

Conditional statements are a fundamental aspect of programming that allow developers to execute specific blocks of code based on certain conditions. In Python, the primary conditional statements used are if, elif, and else. These statements enable coders to implement decision-making capabilities within their programs, guiding the flow of execution based on logical conditions. Understanding the structure and syntax of these statements is crucial for effective programming in Python, as they form the backbone of control flow mechanisms.

The simplest form of a conditional statement in Python begins with the if keyword, followed by a condition and a colon. The block of code that follows must be indented, as Python uses indentation to define the scope of the conditional block. For instance, if you want to check if a variable x is greater than 10, you would write: if x > 10:. This structure allows the code within the block to execute only if the specified condition evaluates to true. This straightforward syntax promotes readability and ease of understanding, which are hallmarks of Python as a programming language.

In addition to basic if statements, Python offers the elif and else keywords to handle multiple conditions effectively. The elif keyword, short for "else if," allows programmers to test additional conditions if the initial if condition is false. This creates a chain of conditions that can be evaluated in sequence. The else keyword serves as a fallback option, executing a block of code when none of the preceding conditions are met. This three-part structure of if, elif, and else provides a robust mechanism for handling various logical scenarios within your programs.

Moreover, Python supports complex conditions using logical operators such as and, or, and not. These operators allow programmers to combine multiple conditions into a single conditional statement, enhancing the flexibility of decision-making in code. For example, you might want to check if a number is both positive and even. By combining conditions using and, you can create a statement like: if x > 0 and x % 2 == 0:. This ability to construct compound conditions expands the potential for creating sophisticated control flows in your applications.

Finally, it is important to follow best practices when using conditional statements to maintain clean and efficient code. Avoid deeply nested conditional statements, which can lead to decreased readability and increased complexity. Instead, consider using functions to encapsulate logic and promote modularity. Additionally, using descriptive variable names and comments can help clarify the purpose of each condition. By adopting these best practices, coders can enhance the maintainability and clarity of their Python code, making it easier for themselves and others to understand and modify in the future.

Looping Structures

Looping structures are fundamental components in Python that facilitate the execution of a block of code multiple times, enhancing the efficiency and conciseness of programs. The two primary looping constructs in Python are the "for" loop and the "while" loop. Each serves its own unique purpose and is suited for different scenarios. Understanding how to effectively use these structures is crucial for any coder, as they enable the automation of repetitive tasks and the handling of collections of data.

The "for" loop in Python is particularly useful for iterating over sequences such as lists, tuples, dictionaries, and strings. By utilizing the "for" loop, programmers can access each element in a sequence without the need for manual indexing. This not only simplifies the code but also reduces the potential for errors associated with off-by-one mistakes. A common use case for a "for" loop is processing items in a list, where each element can be manipulated or analyzed in a straightforward manner. The syntax is simple: "for item in sequence:", which allows for clear and readable code.

On the other hand, the "while" loop continues to execute a block of code as long as a specified condition remains true. This structure is particularly useful when the number of iterations is not predetermined, allowing for more dynamic programming. A typical application of a "while" loop is in scenarios where user input is required, such as prompting a user until they provide valid data. However, caution must be exercised when using "while" loops, as they can lead to infinite loops if the condition is never met, thus creating potential performance issues in the application.

Python also provides control flow statements that can enhance the functionality of loops. The "break" statement allows programmers to exit a loop prematurely, while the "continue" statement skips the current iteration and moves to the next one. These statements can be particularly useful in complex loops where certain conditions may necessitate a change in flow. For instance, in data processing tasks, a programmer may want to skip over invalid entries without terminating the entire loop, thus maintaining the efficiency of the operation.

In addition to the core looping structures, Python's built-in functions can further optimize looping mechanisms. Functions such as "enumerate" and "zip" enable more advanced iteration techniques, allowing for simultaneous looping over multiple sequences and tracking the index of elements. Leveraging these built-in capabilities can lead to cleaner, more efficient code and improve overall readability. By mastering looping structures and their associated functionalities, programmers can significantly enhance their control over data manipulation and flow within their Python applications.

Break and Continue Statements

Break and continue statements are essential control flow mechanisms in Python that allow programmers to manage the execution of loops effectively. The break statement terminates the nearest enclosing loop, whether it is a for loop or a while loop. This functionality is particularly useful in scenarios where a certain condition must be met to exit the loop prematurely. For instance, when searching for an item in a list, a break can be used to stop the loop as soon as the item is found, thus avoiding unnecessary iterations. This not only optimizes performance but also improves code readability by making the intention clear.

On the other hand, the continue statement alters the flow of the loop by skipping the current iteration and moving onto the next one. This is beneficial when you want to ignore specific conditions while processing a dataset. For example, if you are iterating through a list of numbers and want to skip any negative values, you can use continue to bypass those iterations without affecting the remaining numbers. This approach enhances efficiency, especially when working with large datasets where certain values may not be relevant to the intended operation.

Both break and continue statements can be utilized together in a single loop, allowing for more complex control flows. Consider a situation where you are processing user input in a loop. You might want to break out of the loop if the user enters a specific command (like 'exit'), while also using continue to skip over invalid entries. When used judiciously, these statements can lead to cleaner and more maintainable code, as they allow programmers to express the logic of the loop more clearly and directly.

It is important to use break and continue statements with caution, as their misuse can lead to confusing code structures and unintended infinite loops. Always ensure that the conditions leading to a break or continue are well-defined and that they do not conflict with the overall logic of your program. This practice not only adheres to clean coding standards but also aids in debugging by reducing the complexity of loop structures.

In summary, break and continue statements are powerful tools in Python's control flow toolkit, enabling developers to create more efficient and readable loops. By understanding how to implement these statements effectively, programmers can enhance their coding practices and streamline their workflows. As you continue to explore Python's capabilities, mastering these statements will contribute significantly to your ability to write clear and effective code.

Chapter 17: Python Built-in Functions and Libraries

Overview of Built-in Functions

In Python, built-in functions are essential components that enhance the language's functionality and simplify coding tasks. These functions are readily available for use without the need for any additional imports, making them a convenient tool for programmers. The range of built-in functions covers various operations, from mathematical calculations to data type conversions and string manipulations. Understanding how to effectively utilize these functions is crucial for optimizing code efficiency and readability in any Python project.

One of the most significant advantages of built-in functions is their ability to streamline code. Programmers can perform complex tasks using concise, pre-defined functions, which not only reduces the amount of code written but also minimizes the potential for errors. For instance, functions like 'len()' allow developers to quickly determine the length of a list or string, while 'sum()' computes the total of numerical values in an iterable. By leveraging these functions, coders can focus more on the logic and structure of their programs rather than getting bogged down in repetitive coding tasks.

In addition to enhancing code efficiency, built-in functions also contribute to code clarity. When a programmer employs functions such as 'sorted()', 'max()', or 'min()', it communicates the intended operation clearly to anyone reading the code. This clarity is vital in collaborative environments where multiple developers may work on the same project. By using descriptive built-in functions, one can create self-explanatory code that improves maintainability and reduces the learning curve for new team members.

Moreover, built-in functions support various data types, which is a fundamental aspect of Python's versatility. Functions are designed to work seamlessly with different data structures, such as lists, tuples, dictionaries, and sets. For example, the 'type()' function allows programmers to check the data type of a variable, while 'dict()' can create a dictionary from key-value pairs. This adaptability enables developers to handle diverse data manipulations efficiently, catering to the requirements of various applications.

Lastly, understanding built-in functions paves the way for exploring more advanced programming concepts, such as functional programming. Many built-in functions accept other functions as arguments, enabling higher-order programming techniques. Functions like 'map()', 'filter()', and 'reduce()' demonstrate how built-in functions can be combined to create powerful data processing pipelines. Mastering these built-in functions not only enhances a programmer's toolkit but also lays a solid foundation for delving deeper into Python's extensive libraries and frameworks, ultimately leading to more sophisticated and efficient coding practices.

Commonly Used Libraries

In the realm of Python programming, leveraging libraries can significantly enhance productivity and streamline the development process. Libraries are collections of pre-written code that can be imported into a program to perform a variety of tasks, ranging from data manipulation to machine learning. Python boasts a rich ecosystem of libraries that cater to various needs, allowing programmers to avoid reinventing the wheel and focus on solving unique problems. This subchapter will explore some of the most commonly used libraries in Python, highlighting their features and applications.

One of the most popular libraries in Python is NumPy, which provides support for large, multi-dimensional arrays and matrices, along with a collection of mathematical functions to operate on these arrays. NumPy is essential for numerical computations and serves as the foundation for many other libraries, such as SciPy and Pandas. Its ability to perform operations on entire arrays without the need for explicit loops makes it particularly efficient, allowing programmers to write cleaner and more concise code. Understanding NumPy is crucial for coders interested in data analysis and scientific computing.

Pandas is another vital library that has gained immense popularity among data analysts and researchers. It offers data structures like Series and DataFrames, which are designed to handle structured data seamlessly. With Pandas, users can easily manipulate datasets through operations such as filtering, grouping, and aggregating. The library also provides robust tools for reading and writing various file formats, including CSV and Excel, making it a go-to choice for data manipulation tasks. Familiarity with Pandas will enable programmers to efficiently manage and analyze data without extensive boilerplate code.

For those venturing into the field of machine learning, Scikit-learn is an indispensable library that simplifies the implementation of various algorithms. It provides a unified interface for numerous machine learning tasks, including classification, regression, clustering, and dimensionality reduction. Scikit-learn is built on top of NumPy and SciPy, allowing it to leverage their capabilities for efficient data handling and numerical computations. Programmers can quickly prototype machine learning models and perform tasks like cross-validation and hyperparameter tuning, making it a favored choice among both beginners and seasoned data scientists.

In the domain of web development, Flask and Django are two widely adopted frameworks that streamline the creation of web applications. Flask is a micro-framework that offers flexibility and simplicity, making it an excellent option for smaller projects and rapid prototyping. In contrast, Django is a full-featured framework that follows the "batteries included" philosophy, providing a comprehensive suite of tools for building robust web applications. Both frameworks have extensive documentation and a vibrant community, which facilitates learning and problem-solving. Mastering either Flask or Django can greatly enhance a programmer's ability to develop dynamic web applications efficiently.

Importing and Using Libraries

Importing and using libraries in Python is a fundamental skill that enhances the capabilities of your code and streamlines development. Python's extensive standard library offers a range of modules that provide pre-written functions and tools for various tasks, such as file handling, data manipulation, and mathematical operations. By leveraging these libraries, programmers can avoid reinventing the wheel and focus on the unique aspects of their projects. To import a library, you typically use the "import" statement followed by the library's name. This process allows you to access the library's functions and classes, making it essential for efficient coding.

In addition to the standard library, Python supports third-party libraries that can be easily installed and integrated into your projects. These libraries, available through package managers like pip, cover a wide array of functionalities, from web development frameworks like Flask and Django to data analysis libraries like Pandas and NumPy. To install a library, you can simply run a command in your terminal, such as "pip install library_name." Once installed, these libraries can be imported in the same way as standard libraries, providing access to a wealth of additional features that can significantly reduce development time.

Once a library is imported, using its functions is straightforward. Each library typically has its own set of functions and classes that you can call directly. For instance, if you import the math library, you can perform complex mathematical calculations with ease. It is also possible to import specific functions from a library to keep your code clean and efficient, using the syntax "from library_name import function_name." This selective approach not only enhances readability but also minimizes namespace clutter, allowing you to maintain a more organized codebase.

Understanding the documentation for each library is crucial for effective usage. Most libraries come with extensive documentation that outlines available functions, parameters, and usage examples. Familiarizing yourself with this documentation will empower you to utilize the library's features fully and avoid common pitfalls. Additionally, many libraries have an active community that contributes to tutorials and discussions, offering further insights and support for new users.

In conclusion, importing and using libraries is an essential practice for any Python programmer. By utilizing the built-in and third-party libraries available, coders can streamline their workflow, enhance code readability, and leverage powerful functionalities without excessive effort. Mastering the import process and understanding how to navigate library documentation will not only improve coding efficiency but also foster a deeper appreciation for the vast ecosystem of tools available in Python.

Chapter 18: Object-Oriented Programming in Python

Principles of Object-Oriented Programming

Object-Oriented Programming (OOP) is a programming paradigm that uses objects and classes as its core building blocks. In Python, OOP allows for the creation of programs that are modular, reusable, and easy to maintain. The key principles of OOP include encapsulation, inheritance, polymorphism, and abstraction. These principles enable developers to structure their code in a way that promotes clarity and reduces complexity, making it easier to manage large codebases.

Encapsulation is the principle that restricts access to certain components of an object, allowing only controlled interaction with its data and methods. In Python, this is achieved through the use of private and public attributes. By defining attributes as private, you can prevent external code from directly accessing or modifying them, thereby protecting the integrity of the data. Encapsulation also supports the concept of interfaces, where an object can expose certain methods to interact with its internal state without revealing the underlying implementation details.

Inheritance allows one class to inherit attributes and methods from another class, promoting code reuse and the creation of hierarchical relationships between classes. In Python, this can be accomplished using a base class and derived classes. By inheriting from a base class, derived classes can extend or modify the functionality of the base class. This not only reduces redundancy but also helps in maintaining consistency across different parts of an application. The ability to create specialized versions of a class through inheritance is a powerful feature that enhances flexibility in programming.

Polymorphism refers to the ability of different classes to be treated as instances of the same class through a common interface. In Python, this is often achieved through method overriding, where a derived class provides a specific implementation of a method that is already defined in its base class. This allows for dynamic method resolution, where the appropriate method is called based on the object type at runtime. Polymorphism enables developers to write more generic and reusable code, as they can implement functions that work with objects of different classes without knowing their specific types.

Abstraction simplifies complex systems by modeling classes based on essential characteristics while hiding unnecessary details. In Python, abstraction can be implemented using abstract base classes (ABCs), which define a set of methods that must be created within any child class built from the abstract class. This ensures that derived classes adhere to a specific interface, promoting a consistent approach to building applications. By focusing on high-level functionality and hiding implementation details, abstraction helps in reducing complexity and allows programmers to work at a more conceptual level. Understanding and applying these principles of OOP is essential for any coder looking to leverage Python's capabilities effectively.

Creating Classes and Objects

Creating classes and objects is a fundamental aspect of object-oriented programming in Python. A class serves as a blueprint for creating objects, encapsulating data for the object and defining behaviors through methods. By utilizing classes, programmers can model real-world entities and their interactions more intuitively. In Python, defining a class is straightforward, typically using the `class` keyword followed by the class name and a colon. This simplicity allows coders to quickly organize complex data structures and functions into manageable components.

When you create a class, you can include attributes and methods that define the properties and behaviors of the objects instantiated from that class. Attributes are essentially variables that hold data, while methods are functions that perform operations related to the class. For instance, if you have a class representing a car, attributes might include `color`, `make`, and `model`, while methods could include `drive`, `stop`, or `honk`. This encapsulation not only aids in maintaining clean code but also enhances readability and usability, making it easier for other programmers to understand the code structure.

Creating an object from a class is known as instantiation. This is achieved by calling the class name as if it were a function, often passing arguments to the constructor method, typically named `__init__`. This method initializes the object's attributes and prepares it for use. For example, when instantiating a `Car` class, you might call `my_car = Car('red', 'Toyota', 'Corolla')`, which creates an object with specified attributes. The ability to create multiple instances of a class with varying attributes allows for greater flexibility and reusability in your code.

Python also supports inheritance, a powerful feature that allows one class to inherit attributes and methods from another. This capability enables programmers to create a new class that builds upon the existing functionality of an existing class. For example, if you have a base class `Vehicle`, you can create a subclass `Truck` that inherits from `Vehicle` but also adds its own specific attributes and methods. Inheritance promotes code reuse and can simplify the development process, allowing you to build complex systems with less redundancy.

Finally, understanding how to create classes and objects effectively lays the groundwork for mastering Python's object-oriented programming paradigm. By practicing these concepts, programmers can write cleaner, more efficient code that is easier to maintain and scale. As you advance in your Python journey, leveraging classes and objects will enable you to tackle more sophisticated programming challenges, ultimately enhancing your coding proficiency and problem-solving skills in various applications.

Inheritance and Polymorphism

Inheritance and polymorphism are fundamental concepts in object-oriented programming (OOP) that enhance code reusability and flexibility, making them particularly relevant for Python programmers. Inheritance allows a new class, known as a subclass, to inherit attributes and methods from an existing class, referred to as a superclass. This mechanism enables developers to create a hierarchical class structure, making it easier to manage and extend code. By utilizing inheritance, you can avoid redundancy and keep your codebase cleaner, as shared functionality can be written in one place and reused across multiple subclasses.

Python supports multiple inheritance, which means a subclass can derive from more than one superclass. While this feature can lead to powerful class designs, it also introduces complexity, especially when dealing with method resolution order (MRO). When a method is called on an instance of a subclass, Python follows a specific order to determine which method to execute, prioritizing the method in the subclass before looking at its superclasses. Understanding MRO is crucial for avoiding conflicts and ensuring that the correct method is invoked, thus maintaining the integrity of your code.

Polymorphism complements inheritance by allowing objects of different classes to be treated as objects of a common superclass. This means that a single interface can be used with different data types, enabling methods to operate on objects of various classes seamlessly. In

Python, polymorphism is often implemented through method overriding, where a subclass provides a specific implementation of a method that is already defined in its superclass. This capability allows for greater flexibility in programming, as functions can operate on objects of different classes without needing to know their specific types.

The combination of inheritance and polymorphism fosters a more organized and maintainable code structure. For instance, consider a scenario in which you have a superclass called Animal and subclasses like Dog and Cat. Each subclass can implement the method speak() differently, with Dog returning "Bark" and Cat returning "Meow." This design allows you to write functions that can accept any Animal type and call the speak() method, demonstrating how polymorphism can simplify interactions with various objects while leveraging the shared structure provided by inheritance.

To implement these concepts effectively, Python programmers should adopt best practices such as clearly defining class hierarchies and adhering to the single responsibility principle. This approach enhances code readability and ensures that each class has a well-defined purpose. Additionally, utilizing built-in functions and libraries can streamline the implementation of inheritance and polymorphism. By mastering these OOP principles, Python coders can create robust, scalable applications that are easier to maintain and extend.

Chapter 19: Python IDEs and Hot Keys for Efficient Coding

Popular Python IDEs

When it comes to coding in Python, the choice of Integrated Development Environment (IDE) can significantly impact both productivity and the overall coding experience. Popular Python IDEs are specifically designed to provide features that streamline the coding process, making it easier for developers to write, debug, and test their applications. Each IDE offers distinct functionalities, catering to different preferences and project requirements, allowing programmers to choose the best tool for their specific workflow.

One of the most widely used Python IDEs is PyCharm, developed by JetBrains. Known for its robust features, PyCharm provides intelligent code completion, syntax highlighting, and an integrated debugger. Its support for web development frameworks like Django and Flask enhances its appeal to developers working on web applications. The IDE's extensive plugin ecosystem further allows users to customize their environments, making it suitable for both beginners and advanced programmers. Additionally, the built-in support for version control systems simplifies collaborative development.

Another popular choice is Visual Studio Code (VS Code), a lightweight yet powerful code editor developed by Microsoft. With its strong support for Python through extensions, VS Code provides a versatile environment that accommodates various programming languages. It features an integrated terminal, code navigation, and debugging capabilities, making it a favorite among many coders. The ability to customize key bindings and settings allows programmers to tailor their experience, enhancing efficiency and comfort while coding.

For those who prefer a simpler and more straightforward approach, IDLE (Integrated Development and Learning Environment) comes pre-installed with Python. While it may lack some advanced features found in other IDEs, IDLE is user-friendly and ideal for beginners who are just starting to learn Python. Its simplicity allows new programmers to focus on understanding the fundamentals of Python syntax and structure without being overwhelmed by complex tools. IDLE also supports basic features such as syntax highlighting and a built-in debugger.

Spyder is another notable IDE, particularly favored in the scientific and data analysis community. It integrates well with libraries such as NumPy, SciPy, and Matplotlib, making it an excellent choice for data scientists and researchers. Spyder's layout, which includes an interactive console and variable explorer, allows users to visualize and manipulate data effectively. It combines the functionalities of a traditional IDE with the capabilities of scientific computing environments, providing an efficient platform for executing complex data tasks. Each of these IDEs offers unique advantages, ensuring that Python programmers can find a suitable environment to match their coding needs and preferences.

Configuring Your IDE for Productivity

Configuring your Integrated Development Environment (IDE) for productivity is a crucial step in enhancing your coding experience in Python. The right configuration can streamline your workflow, reduce repetitive tasks, and allow you to focus on writing clean and efficient code. Start by selecting an IDE that aligns with your coding style and preferences. Popular choices for Python development include PyCharm, Visual Studio Code, and Jupyter Notebook, each offering unique features that cater to different aspects of Python programming.

Once you have selected your IDE, the next step is to customize its settings to suit your needs. This includes adjusting the layout of the interface, choosing an appropriate color scheme, and setting up the font type and size for better readability. Many IDEs allow you to create custom themes or choose from a variety of pre-installed options, making it easier to work for extended periods without straining your eyes. Additionally, configuring the code editor to automatically format your code according to PEP 8 standards can help maintain consistency and improve code quality.

Hotkeys and keyboard shortcuts play a significant role in enhancing productivity while coding in Python. Familiarizing yourself with the default shortcuts in your chosen IDE can save you precious time. For instance, using shortcuts for common actions like saving files, running scripts, and navigating between files can significantly speed up your workflow. Most IDEs allow you to customize these shortcuts, so take the time to set up key combinations that feel intuitive and comfortable for you, enabling a more fluid coding experience.

Integrating version control systems, such as Git, directly into your IDE can also boost your productivity. Many IDEs provide built-in tools for managing version control, allowing you to commit changes, branch, and merge without leaving your coding environment. This integration simplifies the process of tracking changes in your code and collaborating with other programmers, reducing the friction often associated with using separate tools for version control. Ensure that you familiarize yourself with the version control features available in your IDE to leverage them effectively.

Lastly, consider utilizing plugins and extensions that enhance your IDE's capabilities. These can range from syntax highlighting and code linting tools to more advanced features like code completion and snippets. Extensions can increase efficiency by providing quick access to commonly used code structures, reducing the time spent on repetitive tasks. Always keep your extensions updated to ensure compatibility with the latest features of your IDE and to benefit from ongoing improvements made by the developer community. With the right configuration, your IDE can become an indispensable tool in your Python programming journey, significantly enhancing your productivity.

Keyboard Shortcuts for Efficiency

Keyboard shortcuts can significantly enhance coding efficiency, particularly for those who regularly work in integrated development environments (IDEs) or text editors. In the context of Python programming, familiarizing oneself with these shortcuts can lead to a more streamlined workflow, allowing coders to focus more on logic and less on navigation. Each IDE often comes equipped with a set of default shortcuts that can be customized to fit individual preferences, making it crucial for programmers to explore the options available to them.

Common shortcuts such as copy, paste, and undo are essential, but understanding more specialized shortcuts can unlock a higher level of productivity. For instance, using shortcuts to quickly navigate between files or to jump to specific lines of code can save valuable time during development. In Python, where indentation and structure are paramount, being able to swiftly move through code sections enhances readability and minimizes errors. Familiarizing oneself with these shortcuts can also reduce reliance on the mouse, which can disrupt the flow of coding.

Another area where keyboard shortcuts prove invaluable is during debugging. Many IDEs offer shortcuts that allow developers to set breakpoints, step through code, and evaluate expressions without needing to rely on the mouse. This capability is particularly useful in Python, where understanding the flow of control and identifying issues within loops or functions is often essential for resolving bugs. By mastering these shortcuts, programmers can not only speed up their debugging process but also improve their overall problem-solving skills.

In addition to IDE-specific shortcuts, there are also universal shortcuts applicable across various text editors that can enhance data manipulation tasks in Python. For instance, selecting multiple lines or blocks of code using keyboard shortcuts can facilitate bulk editing, which is particularly useful when dealing with large datasets or extensive scripts. These shortcuts allow for rapid adjustments to variables, data types, or control flow structures, making it easier to adhere to best practices for writing clean and efficient code.

Ultimately, investing time in learning and integrating keyboard shortcuts into daily programming routines can lead to significant long-term benefits. As Python developers continue to engage with more complex projects, the ability to navigate and manipulate code efficiently becomes increasingly important. By leveraging the power of keyboard shortcuts, programmers can enhance their coding experience, streamline their workflows, and ultimately produce higher-quality code in less time.

Chapter 20: Best Practices for Writing Clean Python Code

Code Readability and Style

Code readability and style are essential components of effective programming, particularly in Python, where clear and concise syntax is a hallmark of the language. Readable code improves maintainability not only for the original author but also for others who may work on the code later. Adhering to a consistent style allows developers to quickly understand the purpose and functionality of code segments. This is especially important in collaborative environments, where multiple programmers contribute to a single project. Following established conventions, such as those outlined in PEP 8, can significantly enhance the clarity of Python code.

Indentation plays a crucial role in Python's syntax, directly impacting both readability and functionality. Unlike many programming languages that use braces or keywords to define blocks of code, Python relies on indentation levels. Consequently, consistent use of spaces or tabs is critical. Developers should choose one method of indentation and stick to it throughout the codebase to avoid confusion and potential errors. Many IDEs offer features that automatically manage indentation, which can be a valuable tool for maintaining uniformity and avoiding syntax errors.

Naming conventions also contribute significantly to code readability. Variables, functions, and classes should be named descriptively to reflect their purpose and usage. For instance, using 'calculate_area' instead of a vague name like 'func1' helps convey the function's intent. Additionally, adhering to conventions such as snake_case for variables and functions, and CamelCase for class names, aligns with Python's stylistic guidelines. Clear naming reduces cognitive load, allowing programmers to understand the code more intuitively and facilitating easier debugging and updates.

Commenting and documentation are vital practices that enhance code readability. While well-structured code should be self-explanatory to some extent, comments provide context that can clarify complex logic or reasoning behind specific implementations. However, comments should be used judiciously; over-commenting can clutter the code, making it harder to read. In Python, docstrings serve as a formal way to document modules, classes, and functions. Utilizing these effectively not only enhances readability but also aids in generating automated documentation, which is beneficial for larger projects.

Finally, consistency in code style reinforces readability across projects and teams. Adopting style guides, such as PEP 8, and utilizing automated tools like linters can help ensure that code adheres to best practices. By embracing a consistent approach to code structure, variable naming, and documentation, programmers can produce cleaner, more maintainable code. This not only improves individual productivity but also fosters a culture of quality within teams, ultimately leading to more robust and reliable software solutions.

Documentation and Comments

Documentation and comments are essential components of writing clean and maintainable Python code. They serve as a guide not only for the original author but also for others who may read or modify the code in the future. In Python, documentation can take various forms, including docstrings, comments, and external documentation files. Each of these elements plays a vital role in enhancing the readability and usability of the code by providing context and explanations for the logic and structure.

Docstrings are a specific type of documentation string that describes a module, class, method, or function. They are written directly below the definition of the element they describe and are enclosed in triple quotes. This convention allows for easy access to documentation through Python's built-in help system. By writing clear and concise docstrings, you can communicate the purpose, parameters, return values, and any exceptions that may be raised by your functions. This practice not only aids other developers but also serves as a self-reminder of the function’s intent when revisiting the code after some time.

Comments, on the other hand, are informal annotations within the code that clarify complex logic or decisions. In Python, comments begin with a hash symbol (#) and continue to the end of the line. They can be used to explain why certain approaches were taken, outline the steps in a complex algorithm, or provide warnings about potential pitfalls. While writing comments, it's important to strike a balance; they should be used judiciously to avoid cluttering the code. Over-commenting can obscure the logic rather than clarify it, while under-commenting can leave readers confused about the code's intent.

To maintain high-quality documentation and comments, developers should adhere to best practices. Comments should be clear, relevant, and concise, ideally explaining the 'why' rather than the 'what' of the code, as the latter should be evident from the code itself. Additionally, consistency in style and terminology is crucial for maintaining a coherent documentation standard across the entire project. When possible, leverage tools such as linters and formatters that can help enforce these standards, ensuring that the documentation remains an integral part of the coding process.

In conclusion, the significance of documentation and comments in Python programming cannot be overstated. They not only facilitate easier maintenance and collaboration but also contribute to the overall quality of the code. By prioritizing well-structured docstrings and meaningful comments, programmers can enhance the understanding and longevity of their projects. As Python continues to evolve, adhering to these practices ensures that code remains accessible and efficient, aligning with the best practices for writing clean code and facilitating effective collaboration within development teams.

Refactoring and Code Reviews

Refactoring and code reviews are essential practices in software development that contribute significantly to code quality and maintainability. Refactoring involves restructuring existing code without changing its external behavior, aiming to improve readability, reduce complexity, and enhance performance. In Python, where readability is a core principle, refactoring allows programmers to streamline their code and make it more intuitive. Techniques such as simplifying complex functions, renaming variables for clarity, and breaking down large modules into smaller, reusable components are fundamental in the refactoring process. By focusing on these aspects, developers can create a more efficient codebase that is easier to navigate and modify in the future.

Code reviews serve as a critical checkpoint in the development process, allowing programmers to evaluate each other's code before it is merged into a shared codebase. This collaborative practice not only fosters knowledge sharing among team members but also helps identify potential issues early in the development cycle. During a code review, reviewers examine aspects such as code structure, adherence to Python's PEP 8 style guidelines, and the use of appropriate data types and control flow mechanisms. Engaging in code reviews promotes a culture of continuous improvement, where developers learn from one another and adopt best practices for writing clean, efficient code.

Both refactoring and code reviews align closely with the principles of writing clean Python code. By regularly refactoring code, developers can eliminate technical debt, which accumulates when shortcuts are taken in the coding process. This practice encourages the use of Python's built-in functions and libraries effectively, reducing redundancy and improving overall performance. Additionally, code reviews help ensure that the code adheres to established conventions and standards, such as proper variable naming and consistent indentation. These practices collectively contribute to a more manageable codebase, ultimately leading to higher productivity and fewer bugs.

In the context of object-oriented programming in Python, refactoring can also enhance the design of classes and their interactions. By applying design patterns and principles such as encapsulation and inheritance, developers can create more modular and reusable code. Refactoring allows for the identification of unnecessary dependencies and can lead to a more coherent class structure. Code reviews in this domain become crucial as they help ensure that the object-oriented principles are applied correctly and that the code remains flexible for future changes or enhancements.

When utilizing integrated development environments (IDEs) for Python, tools and features often support both refactoring and code review processes. Many IDEs provide hotkeys for common refactoring operations, such as renaming variables or extracting methods, making it easier for programmers to improve their code without extensive manual effort. Additionally, some IDEs have built-in code review functionalities that facilitate commenting and discussion on specific lines of code. By leveraging these tools, coders can enhance their workflow and ensure that both refactoring and code reviews are integral parts of their coding practices, leading to the development of robust, high-quality Python applications.

Chapter 21: Common Python Shortcuts for Data Manipulation

Data Structures in Python

Data structures in Python are fundamental building blocks that allow programmers to organize and manage data efficiently. Python provides several built-in data structures, each designed to cater to specific types of data manipulation needs. The most commonly used data structures include lists, tuples, sets, and dictionaries. Understanding these structures is crucial for any coder looking to write clean and efficient code, as they directly influence performance and readability.

Lists in Python are one of the most versatile data structures, capable of holding an ordered collection of items. They can contain elements of different data types, including other lists, and allow for dynamic resizing. Coders can easily add, remove, or modify elements in a list using various built-in methods such as append, remove, or insert. Lists also support slicing, which enables programmers to access sub-portions of the data, making it easier to manipulate large datasets efficiently.

Tuples, on the other hand, are immutable sequences, meaning that once a tuple is created, its contents cannot be altered. This immutability makes tuples ideal for storing data that should not change throughout the lifecycle of an application. Tuples are often used in situations where data integrity is essential, such as storing fixed configurations or returning multiple values from a function. Their lightweight nature makes tuples faster and more memory-efficient compared to lists, which is a crucial consideration for high-performance applications.

Sets offer a unique approach to data handling by providing an unordered collection of unique elements. This property makes sets particularly useful for operations that require the elimination of duplicates or the need to perform mathematical set operations, such as union and intersection. Python's set operations are implemented with high efficiency, allowing programmers to work with large datasets without significant performance degradation. Utilizing sets can simplify code and enhance clarity, especially when dealing with large volumes of data where uniqueness is a critical requirement.

Dictionaries, or associative arrays, are powerful data structures that store key-value pairs. This allows for fast lookups and efficient data retrieval based on keys. Coders can use dictionaries to represent complex data relationships, such as mapping user IDs to user profiles or storing configuration settings. The ability to nest dictionaries also provides a way to create complex data structures that can model real-world situations more accurately. Mastering the use of these data structures is essential for programmers aiming to write clean, efficient, and maintainable Python code.

List Comprehensions and Lambda Functions

List comprehensions and lambda functions are two powerful features in Python that enhance the efficiency and readability of code. List comprehensions provide a concise way to create lists by iterating over an iterable and applying an expression to each item. Instead of using traditional loops, which can often lead to verbose and less readable code, list comprehensions enable developers to generate lists in a single line. The syntax is straightforward: it consists of an expression followed by a `for` clause, and optionally, one or more `if` clauses to filter items. This approach not only simplifies code but also improves performance in many cases.

Lambda functions, or anonymous functions, are another essential aspect of Python that complement list comprehensions. They allow programmers to create small, unnamed functions at runtime, primarily used for short operations that are not reused elsewhere. The syntax of a lambda function consists of the `lambda` keyword followed by a list of parameters, a colon, and an expression. This lightweight function is particularly useful when paired with functions like `map()`, `filter()`, and `reduce()`, enabling developers to apply operations on iterables without formally defining a function. The use of lambda functions can lead to clearer and more concise code, especially in functional programming paradigms.

When combined, list comprehensions and lambda functions significantly streamline data manipulation tasks. For instance, using a lambda function within a list comprehension allows for the transformation of data in a single, readable line. This combination is often seen in scenarios where data needs to be processed or filtered based on specific criteria. For example, one could use a lambda function to square numbers in a list while simultaneously filtering out negative values, showcasing the elegance and power of using these two features together.

Efficiency is not the only benefit of using list comprehensions and lambda functions. Their integration into Python's syntax encourages best practices for writing clean code. By reducing the amount of boilerplate code needed, developers can focus on the logic and functionality of their applications rather than getting bogged down in syntax. Furthermore, this approach aligns well with Python's philosophy of readability and simplicity, making code easier to understand and maintain, which is crucial for collaborative projects and long-term codebases.

In conclusion, mastering list comprehensions and lambda functions is vital for any Python developer aiming to write efficient and clean code. These tools not only enhance coding efficiency but also align with best practices for data manipulation and control flow. By leveraging these features, programmers can improve both the performance and readability of their code, ultimately leading to more maintainable and effective programming solutions. Embracing these concepts will undoubtedly elevate a coder's proficiency in Python and contribute positively to their overall coding journey.

Using Pandas for Data Manipulation

Pandas is a powerful library in Python that offers flexible and efficient data manipulation capabilities, making it an essential tool for coders and computer programmers. At its core, Pandas provides two primary data structures: Series and DataFrames. A Series is a one-dimensional labeled array capable of holding any data type, while a DataFrame is a two-dimensional labeled data structure with columns of potentially different types. Understanding these structures is crucial, as they serve as the foundation for data manipulation tasks, allowing users to easily handle, analyze, and visualize data.

One of the key features of Pandas is its ability to read and write data from various file formats, including CSV, Excel, and SQL databases. The `read_csv()` function is particularly popular for importing tabular data into a DataFrame, while `to_csv()` allows for exporting data back into a CSV format. These functions streamline the process of data ingestion and output, making it easier for programmers to transition between data sources and maintain a smooth workflow. Leveraging these built-in methods not only saves time but also reduces the likelihood of errors that can occur when manually handling data files.

Data manipulation in Pandas is also facilitated by its extensive set of methods for filtering, sorting, and aggregating data. For instance, the `loc[]` and `iloc[]` functions enable programmers to access specific rows and columns based on labels or integer positions, respectively. Pandas also supports boolean indexing, which allows for filtering data based on conditions. Functions such as `groupby()` are essential for aggregating data, enabling users to compute statistics like sums, averages, or counts across different categories. This flexibility in data manipulation is vital for conducting exploratory data analysis and deriving insights from datasets.

In addition to these fundamental operations, Pandas provides robust capabilities for handling missing data and performing data transformations. The `fillna()` method can be used to replace missing values with specific values or methods, while `dropna()` can remove any rows or columns with missing entries. Furthermore, the `apply()` function allows users to apply custom functions to DataFrame columns, facilitating complex transformations and calculations. This versatility makes Pandas an invaluable resource for data cleaning and preparation, which are often critical steps in any data analysis process.

Lastly, integrating Pandas with other Python libraries enhances its data manipulation capabilities even further. For example, combining Pandas with NumPy allows for efficient numerical operations, while using it alongside Matplotlib or Seaborn can facilitate effective data visualization. Programmers can also utilize Jupyter Notebooks for an interactive coding experience, which is particularly beneficial for prototyping and exploring data. By mastering the use of Pandas, coders can significantly improve their data manipulation skills, making their analyses more robust and their workflows more efficient.

Chapter 22: Python Quiz

Testing Your Knowledge

Testing your knowledge is a critical step in mastering the essentials of Python programming. This process not only reinforces your understanding of Python's syntax but also enhances your ability to apply concepts effectively in real-world scenarios. Engaging with various testing methods can help solidify your grasp of key topics such as data types, variables, control flow, and object-oriented programming principles. By actively challenging yourself with exercises and practical applications, you can transform theoretical knowledge into practical proficiency.

One effective way to test your knowledge is through coding challenges that focus on Python's core basics and hot keys. Websites like LeetCode, HackerRank, and Codewars offer a plethora of problems that range from beginner to advanced levels. These platforms allow you to apply Python's syntax and structure in a competitive format, helping you to identify areas for improvement. As you solve problems, pay attention to the efficiency of your solutions, as well as the language features you employ, such as list comprehensions and built-in functions, which are pivotal in writing clean and efficient code.

Furthermore, understanding data types and variables is fundamental in Python. Testing your knowledge through quizzes and interactive exercises can provide instant feedback on your comprehension of concepts like integers, floats, strings, and lists. You can also create small projects that require you to manipulate and analyze data using these types. For instance, writing a program that processes user input to categorize data or perform calculations can deepen your understanding of how variables interact. Such hands-on experience is invaluable for grasping the nuances of Python's data handling capabilities.

Control flow and looping mechanisms are vital components of Python that dictate the behavior of your code. To test your understanding of these concepts, consider engaging in exercises that require you to implement conditional statements and loops effectively. Building simple applications, such as a text-based game or a data processing script, can challenge your ability to utilize if-else conditions and iterative constructs. Additionally, experimenting with different looping techniques, such as for loops and while loops, will enhance your problem-solving skills and reinforce your understanding of program flow.

Finally, exploring object-oriented programming (OOP) in Python is essential for writing scalable and maintainable code. To solidify your knowledge in this area, create classes and objects based on real-world scenarios and test their functionality through various methods. Engaging in peer code reviews can also provide insights into best practices for structuring your code. By regularly testing your skills and seeking feedback, you can refine your approach to Python programming, optimize your coding practices, and ultimately become a more proficient and confident coder.

Build Your First Python Program

To build your first Python program, you will start by setting up your development environment. Python is highly versatile and can be run on various platforms such as Windows, macOS, and Linux. The first step involves downloading the latest version of Python from the official website. Once installed, choose an integrated development environment (IDE) that suits your needs. Popular options include PyCharm, Visual Studio Code, and Jupyter Notebook. These environments provide features like syntax highlighting, code completion, and built-in debugging tools that enhance coding efficiency.

After setting up your IDE, you can create a new Python file, typically with a .py extension. Begin your program by writing a simple script that prints "Hello, World!" to the console. This classic example introduces you to the syntax of Python. In Python, printing to the console can be achieved using the print() function, which requires parentheses around the string you wish to output. Understanding this foundational element of Python syntax sets the stage for more complex programming tasks.

Next, explore Python's data types and variables. In Python, you can create variables without explicitly declaring their types, as Python is dynamically typed.

For instance, you can assign a string to a variable and later assign an integer to the same variable without any issues. This flexibility allows for rapid prototyping and experimentation. To illustrate, you could modify your initial program to include a variable for the user's name, allowing you to personalize the greeting. This step highlights the importance of understanding data types, such as strings, integers, and lists.

Once you have a basic program functioning, you can enhance its interactivity by incorporating user input. The input() function allows you to receive user data from the console. By prompting the user to enter their name and then using that input in your print statement, you create a more dynamic experience. This introduces control flow concepts, as you can use conditional statements to alter the program's behavior based on user input, laying the groundwork for more complex logic in future projects.

Finally, as you continue to develop your Python skills, familiarize yourself with best practices for writing clean and efficient code. This includes following naming conventions, using comments to document your code, and breaking your program into functions to enhance readability and reusability. Learning how to utilize built-in functions and libraries will also streamline your coding process, enabling you to leverage existing code for common tasks. Through this structured approach, building your first Python program not only provides a hands-on introduction to the language but also establishes a solid foundation for mastering Python programming in the long run.

Additional References

In this subchapter on "Additional References," we aim to provide a curated list of resources that will enhance your understanding of Python's syntax, data types, and variable management. These references encompass a variety of materials, including books, online documentation, tutorials, and community forums, all of which are invaluable for coders and computer programmers seeking to deepen their knowledge of Python. Each reference has been selected for its relevance to core Python concepts, offering insights into best practices, coding efficiency, and advanced features.

One of the most authoritative resources is the official Python documentation, which offers comprehensive coverage of Python's syntax and built-in functions. This resource is essential for understanding how to leverage the language effectively, from basic constructs to more advanced topics like object-oriented programming. The documentation includes numerous examples and explanations that elucidate Python's behavior, making it a go-to reference for coders at all levels. It is frequently updated, ensuring that you have access to the latest information and practices.

For those interested in structured learning, "Automate the Boring Stuff with Python" by Al Sweigart is highly recommended. This book focuses on practical applications of Python, teaching you how to write programs that automate everyday tasks. It covers fundamental concepts while providing real-world examples that demonstrate the power of Python's syntax and its data manipulation capabilities. This resource is particularly beneficial for those who prefer a hands-on approach to learning and want to see immediate applications of their coding skills.

Online platforms such as Codecademy and Coursera offer interactive courses tailored to Python programming. These platforms provide guided learning experiences that include quizzes and projects to reinforce understanding of Python syntax, control flow, and data types. The interactive nature of these courses allows you to practice coding in real-time, fostering a deeper comprehension of material through immediate application. Engaging with these platforms can significantly enhance your coding efficiency and familiarity with Python's built-in libraries.

Finally, community forums such as Stack Overflow and Reddit's r/learnpython are excellent for seeking help and sharing knowledge. These platforms allow you to connect with fellow programmers, ask questions, and share insights about Python coding challenges. Engaging with the community can provide practical tips and shortcuts that contribute to writing clean, efficient code. Utilizing these additional references will empower you to master Python programming, streamline your coding process, and ensure that you are well-equipped to tackle various programming tasks.

www.ingramcontent.com/pod-product-compliance
Lightning Source LLC
LaVergne TN
LVHW062149200926
848484LV00007B/1887